ALECKY BLYTHE

In 2003, Alecky founded Recorded Delivery, whose first production, *Come Out Eli*, premiered at the Arcola Theatre, London, and later transferred to the BAC (winner of the Time Out Award for Best Performance on the Fringe). The company went on to make *All the Right People Come Here* (New Wimbledon Theatre). Alecky has since created *Strawberry Fields* (The Courtyard, Hereford); *Cruising* (Bush Theatre, London); *The Girlfriend Experience* (Royal Court Theatre and Young Vic, London); *I Only Came Here for Six Months* (KVS and Les Halles, Brussels); and *Do We Look Like Refugees?!*, a joint project for the National Theatre Studio and the Rustaveli Theatre, Georgia (Assembly Rooms, Edinburgh Festival Fringe, 2010; winner of Fringe First Award). Alecky was one of the writers on *Decade* (Headlong) and co-wrote *Friday Night Sex* with Michael Wynne (Royal Court). *London Road*, with music composed by Adam Cork, premiered at the Cottesloe auditorium of the National Theatre in 2011 (winner of Best Musical, Critics' Circle Awards) and transferred to the Olivier auditorium in 2012.

For television she has written *A Man in a Box* (IWC and Channel 4); *The Riots: In Their Own Words* (BBC2).

For film she has adapted *London Road* into a feature (BBC Film, BFI, National Theatre).

Other Titles in this Series

Mike Bartlett
BULL
AN INTERVENTION
KING CHARLES III

Tom Basden
HOLES
JOSEPH K
THERE IS A WAR

Alecky Blythe
CRUISING
THE GIRLFRIEND EXPERIENCE
LONDON ROAD *with* Adam Cork

Jez Butterworth
JERUSALEM
JEZ BUTTERWORTH PLAYS: ONE
MOJO
THE NIGHT HERON
PARLOUR SONG
THE RIVER
THE WINTERLING

Caryl Churchill
BLUE HEART
CHURCHILL PLAYS: THREE
CHURCHILL PLAYS: FOUR
CHURCHILL: SHORTS
CLOUD NINE
DING DONG THE WICKED
A DREAM PLAY *after* Strindberg
DRUNK ENOUGH TO SAY
    I LOVE YOU?
FAR AWAY
HOTEL
ICECREAM
LIGHT SHINING IN
    BUCKINGHAMSHIRE
LOVE AND INFORMATION
MAD FOREST
A NUMBER
SEVEN JEWISH CHILDREN
THE SKRIKER
THIS IS A CHAIR
THYESTES *after* Seneca
TRAPS

Elinor Cook
THE GIRL'S GUIDE TO SAVING
    THE WORLD

Stella Feehily
BANG BANG BANG
DREAMS OF VIOLENCE
DUCK
O GO MY MAN
THIS MAY HURT A BIT

debbie tucker green
BORN BAD
DIRTY BUTTERFLY
NUT
RANDOM
STONING MARY
TRADE & GENERATIONS
TRUTH AND RECONCILIATION

Nancy Harris
LOVE IN A GLASS JAR
NO ROMANCE
OUR NEW GIRL

Vicky Jones
THE ONE

Dawn King
CIPHERS
FOXFINDER

Lucy Kirkwood
BEAUTY AND THE BEAST
    with Katie Mitchell
BLOODY WIMMIN
CHIMERICA
HEDDA *after* Ibsen
IT FELT EMPTY WHEN THE
    HEART WENT AT FIRST BUT
    IT IS ALRIGHT NOW
NSFW
TINDERBOX

Conor McPherson
DUBLIN CAROL
McPHERSON PLAYS: ONE
McPHERSON PLAYS: TWO
McPHERSON PLAYS: THREE
THE NIGHT ALIVE
PORT AUTHORITY
THE SEAFARER
SHINING CITY
THE VEIL
THE WEIR

Chloë Moss
CHRISTMAS IS MILES AWAY
HOW LOVE IS SPELT
FATAL LIGHT
THE GATEKEEPER
THE WAY HOME
THIS WIDE NIGHT

Bruce Norris
CLYBOURNE PARK
THE LOW ROAD
THE PAIN AND THE ITCH
PURPLE HEART

Evan Placey
GIRLS LIKE THAT
PRONOUN

Jack Thorne
2ND MAY 1997
BUNNY
BURYING YOUR BROTHER IN THE
    PAVEMENT
LET THE RIGHT ONE IN
    after John Ajvide Lindqvist
MYDIDAE
STACY & FANNY AND FAGGOT
WHEN YOU CURE ME

Phoebe Waller-Bridge
FLEABAG

Alecky Blythe

LITTLE REVOLUTION

NICK HERN BOOKS

London

www.nickhernbooks.co.uk

A Nick Hern Book

Little Revolution first published in Great Britain as a paperback original in 2014 by Nick Hern Books Limited, The Glasshouse, 49a Goldhawk Road, London W12 8QP

Little Revolution copyright © 2014 Alecky Blythe

Alecky Blythe has asserted her right to be identified as the author of this work

Cover image concept by NB Studio
Photograph by Bruno Drummond

Designed and typeset by Nick Hern Books, London
Printed in the UK by CPI Group (UK) Ltd

A CIP catalogue record for this book is available from the British Library

ISBN   978 1 84842 432 6

MIX
Paper from
responsible sources
FSC® C013604
www.fsc.org

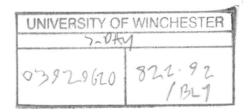

Interview with Alecky Blythe

Chris Lawson, the Almeida Theatre's Schools and Education Manager, spoke with playwright Alecky Blythe about the process of taking the production from the streets to the stage.

As the show is a piece of verbatim theatre, could you explain the technique, what it involves, and how it is different to the more traditional way of scripting a play?

Nothing in this play is written or made up. All the words that the actors speak are words that I have collected with my Dictaphone. I do interviews with real-life people in real-life situations which I record, and then I edit them, so the actors are all portraying people that I've met. They say the words that I've collected – not just what a person has said, but also with the original accent, intonation, delivery and speech pattern with all the details.

What was your first encounter with verbatim work, and what encouraged you to continue using the technique for your plays?

I was introduced to verbatim work by a director called Mark Wing-Davey. He used to teach a course when he was running the Actors Centre in London. He taught me this particular performance technique, which I took to and went off to make my own show – and I haven't stopped since.

Little Revolution *is based on your recordings from the London Riots in 2011 – and more specifically, the riots in Hackney. Why did you decide to use the riots as your starting point? How did you approach it?*

I like to get material which is lively and spontaneous rather than sitting down in a situation which is set up more formally. I often feel that I get my best material in an event, when people are not so focused on the fact that there's someone with a microphone in front of them. Even though they know they're being recorded, if they are out watching something – a riot or a siege on a street – they may be a little more relaxed. I could see on the news when members of the public were out; it was an event that I could go to and a big talking point that people would have strong opinions on. The riots were something that lots of people were affected by, therefore [I knew] there would be lots of material to collect about it.

Did you ever have any concerns for your own safety?

Yes, at certain points. There's a point in the show when I go out on the night that the riots hit in Hackney, and I end up literally ten yards away from a shop which is getting looted. I was talking to the locals and thinking, 'Maybe one day this might end up as a play, you never know' – but a lot of things that I start recording don't make it onto the stage – I thought I'd take some pictures for the set designer; it might have come in handy. I was trying to take general shots of the scene, like burning cars. I was taking a photo as someone came out of the looted convenience store with a crate of beer or something and he thought I was taking a picture of him and started asking me who I was working for, what was I doing… I thought he was going to grab my camera off me, which was on my phone. But he actually politely asked me to scroll through my photos so he could check he wasn't in any of them – and as it was, his head was not in the shot, so he was completely fine about it! But I was kind of terrified…

So did you delete the photo?

No, he didn't ask me to because his face wasn't in it! It was literally neck down so he was like, 'Okay, fine, go back, go back again, okay.' And off he went! He was polite, but it was dark and I was scared. And I was picked up with excitement, as a lot of people were, which is why they went out – not just to loot but to watch. There was a weird, false sense of security because they weren't attacking people. I knew I was getting good material because I was talking to the people who were watching and stuff. You just get caught up in the wake of it.

It sounds like you stayed there for quite a long time to get so much material. How did you decide what would make it into the show?

Well, after that night I went back to the one particular shop I saw get looted – and there were loads of people there: people who lived in the area, the media... I met the shopkeeper and heard about this fund that was being set up for him, and from that point I could see that there was this narrative. I'd been to Tottenham, to Croydon and other places, but at some point you do have to narrow things down and kind of go, 'Okay, maybe it's the story of this guy's shop and what happens to it.' So that's the story that I followed.

So you met the shopkeeper, and you've told us about the guy who politely asked you to show him your photos. Were there any other characters who particularly stood out for you? Were there people that you met that you found particularly fascinating?

Absolutely, and they tend to be the protagonists in the piece. Verbatim relies so much on building a relationship with people, so the people I found fascinating or had a rapport with were the people I revisited. There's a lovely couple called Sarah and Tony who were instrumental in helping to get Siva's shop back up and running. I found them not only fascinating but also instrumental in the story. It's great when those two things come together.

Likewise, there's a very sage barber on the street called Colin who's a great philosopher. I'd go to him and he'd give me his insight; given that he'd had his shop there for twenty years he's familiar with that area. On one side of the road you've got a lovely square and on the other side there's quite a big estate, so there're quite contrasting people living on the two sides of the street. Colin had seen the changing face of the area. In a way, there are too many characters to mention!

Before rehearsals started, Almeida Projects spent several weeks recruiting thirty-four participants to become a community chorus made up of volunteers, predominantly from Hackney, Islington and other London boroughs. What is the role of the community chorus in the show?

The community chorus is incredibly important and we *definitely* couldn't do the show without them. It was a great idea that the theatre came up with for us to do it in this way. So, because there're quite a few scenes which require a lot of bodies onstage, a lot of action – you've got the riots then there's also a big tea party, and when the shop was reopened a party was held to celebrate. The community chorus allows us to hopefully tell the story in a much clearer way and helps it to feel more like the authentic city that it is. It is peopled with lots of beings, basically. The community chorus are very integrated into the scenes with the professional actors. This is when the play really comes alive as you've got people from a wide variety of backgrounds coming together which reflects a central theme within the piece.

Has creating Little Revolution *changed how you think about community?*

I think it has. It's made me realise that you can be living in one community but there are massive divisions in it – it's almost like living parallel lives really, even though they're in the same postcode. The residents [of the community in the play] all use the same shop – the one that got looted – to get their bottled water and Oyster cards, but they are living very different lives. I think some communities are perhaps fractured and getting more fractured as the divide between rich and poor grows and gentrification continues. And fantastic initiatives like the tea party will still be criticised if people feel that the ideas are not coming from their side of the street.

Kind of a Catch-22.

Exactly.

Finally, you're actually performing in Little Revolution. *What does it mean for a writer to perform in their show?*

It's great! I'm very excited, but I am terrified of course. I am playing me so hopefully I will be able to pull that off... It's not like it'll be my first time onstage however, but it's one thing to put on a mask and play someone else and it's another to show your hand and play yourself. It's quite revealing for me which is always a little bit daunting.

But what I'm looking forward to is that often as a writer, the play opens and you just have to sit in the audience and watch it, and they're all up there onstage having a great time, hanging out in the dressing rooms and I always feel like I want to be part of that community! So now it's nice that I can sort of see it through and be in it until it ends, which will be great.

Little Revolution was first performed at the Almeida Theatre, London, on 26 August 2014. The cast was as follows:

JANE/VARIOUS	Ronni Ancona
SADIE/VARIOUS	Melanie Ash
ALECKY	Alecky Blythe
KYLE/VARIOUS	Bayo Gbadamosi
FATHER ROB/VARIOUS	Lloyd Hutchinson
SIVA	Rez Kempton
IAN/VARIOUS	Barry McCarthy
COLIN/VARIOUS	Lucian Msamati
DEANNE/VARIOUS	Clare Perkins
TONY/VARIOUS	Michael Shaeffer
SARAH/VARIOUS	Imogen Stubbs
ALAN DEIN/VARIOUS	Rufus Wright

COMMUNITY CHORUS

Alexander Akosile, Stephan Bolompa, Jason Borley, Sally Charlton, Rose-Marie Christian, Sarita Gabony, Ben Gardner, Ingrid Nixie Greep, Jessica Hammett, Stephen Harrison, Rasfan Haval, Miriam Hoenig, Kizzie Hopkinson, Kamal Karimullah, Don Kunga, Lauren La Rocque, Chris Lib, Lesley Lingwood, Joshua Lyster-Downer, Timesha Mathurin, Corey Montague-Sholay, Zena Peter, Tyra Porter, Jason Primus, Ramelle Reid, Nabhaan Rizwan, María Cristina Salcedo Gómez, Amania Scott-Samuels, Christopher Sherwood, Naz Simsek, Abrar Wakeel

Director	Joe Hill-Gibbins
Set Designer	Ian MacNeil
Costume Designer	Holly Waddington
Lighting Designer	Guy Hoare
Sound Designer	Paul Arditti
Movement Director	Imogen Knight
Casting	Joyce Nettles
Associate Director	Rebecca Hill
Costume Supervisor	Jackie Orton
Community Chorus Assistant Director	Chris Lawson
Design Assistant	Jim Gaffney
Movement Assistant	Jenny Ogilvie

Characters
in order of appearance

ALECKY, *writer*
GIRL WHO SAYS NO
GASMAN
ROMANIAN MAN
WELDER JOHN

TONY, *local resident and
    member of the Clapton
    Square Users Group*
FATHER ROB, *Vicar of St
    John at Hackney*
SARAH, *local resident and
    member of the Clapton
    Square Users Group.
    Married to Tony*
ALAN DEIN, *BBC journalist*
IAN RATHBONE, *local
    councillor*
SIVA, *owner of Clarence
    Road Convenience Store*
JANE, *local resident*

BLING GIRL 1
BLING GIRL 2
BLING GIRL 3
TURKISH SHOPKEEPER
BOY 1 IN BASEBALL CAP
BOY 2 IN BASEBALL CAP
SHOCKED MAN
HINDREY ROAD MUM,
    *woman from Pembury
    estate*
KATE, *mother from Pembury
    estate*

VARIOUS RIOTERS
SAM
LOOTER 1
LOOTER 2

LUKE, *boy from Pembury
    estate*
BOY ON BIKE
LUKE'S MUM, *woman from
    Pembury estate*
MALTESE MAN
SHUTTER WOMAN
DEANNE
OLDER NORTHERN
    WOMAN
YOUNG NORTHERN
    WOMAN
AMERICAN JOURNALIST
PLAIN-CLOTHES
    POLICEMAN
HEIDI, *journalist with the
    Hackney Herald*

STEVE LORD, *Pembury
    estate resident and
    chairman of the Pembury
    Tenants' Association*
DOT, *Pembury estate
    resident*
KYLE
COLIN THE BARBER
SEVEN-POUND CLIENT
REEVES CORNER
    WOMAN 1

REEVES CORNER
   WOMAN 2
JEROME
TYRONE
SADIE, *mother from Pembury*
   estate
MAN AT MEETING

M&S EMPLOYEE
CHRISTOPH, *journalist for*
   Der Spiegel *magazine*
OFFICIAL
   PHOTOGRAPHER
GUEST SHOPKEEPER
SKIN CLIENT

WOMAN IN BARBER'S
GIRL ONLOOKER 1
BOY ONLOOKER 1
BOY ONLOOKER 2
GIRL ONLOOKER 2
MAN ONLOOKER 1
MAN ONLOOKER 2
MAN ONLOOKER 3
POLICEMAN 1
POLICEMAN 2
HULA-HOOP GIRL
MAN WITH CAKE
MC POWER

Note on the Text

A forward slash in the text (/) indicates the point at which the next speaker interrupts.

Inconsistencies in spelling and grammar are deliberate and indicate idiosyncracies in the speech and delivery of the characters.

Author's Note

Some names have been changed.

Special thanks to everyone who generously shared their stories.

A.B.

This text went to press before the end of rehearsals and so may differ slightly from the play as performed.

SECTION 1 – Riots and Steering Group

1. Riots Part 1

The real audio plays over the PA. Helicopters can be heard in the distance.

ALECKY (*PA*). Okay. Hackney.

Hackney.

On Monday the 8th.

After…

Tottenham.

Half-lines heard from people in the street in the background:

VOICES (*PA*). Someone's put uh…

…ah yeah.

Have you been out?… No I haven't… yeah.

…three that they smashed up actually and took the…

The clock is boarded up.

Laughter.

ALECKY (*PA*). I don't s'pose I can speak to any of you? I make documentary plays, and I record conversations on here.

GIRL WHO SAYS NO (*PA*). I don't wanna be on TV it's / alright.

ALECKY (*PA*). / No it's not a TV.

GIRL WHO SAYS NO (*PA*). Oh.

ALECKY (*PA*). Oh it's just your voice would I be able to record your voice no names no pictures no I b–… What I do I is I – speak to people – no? Okay.

Half-lines heard in the soundscape:

I'm / – make documentary plays, can I talk to you for two // minutes.

GASMAN. / I'm. // I'm the gas board. I'm gas board, I'm not police.

ALECKY (*PA*). Ah ha.

GASMAN. I'm just 'ere, I'm just 'ere doing a gas job.

More voices and helicopter are heard.

ALECKY (*PA*). Can I talk to you? I make plays. I'm a writer.

ROMANIAN MAN (*PA*). Sorry?

ALECKY (*PA*). I'm a play– I write for the theatre –

ROMANIAN MAN (*PA*). Yeah.

ALECKY (*PA*). – And I record conversations on here with people.

ROMANIAN MAN (*PA*). Ahh so for interview… / Like that.

ALECKY (*PA*). / Yeah. Can I do interview with you? // (*Beat*.) No?

During the course of the speech the PA fades and the actor playing the ROMANIAN MAN *is left speaking, unassisted.*

ROMANIAN MAN. // I'm foreigner I don't know honestly, I don't know. I'm so sorry. I'm – amazing some time because, in my life I don't see like dat. Ha I don't know why but, no never like dat, I don't see in my life like dat, honestly, it's the first time for me. I'm coorious honestly – Yes-yes. I'm little bit scary-ed but, I dunno because in my country, never like dat. Never like dat. Honestly I-I want to buy one pack of cigarette but all the-the shops is closed so I dunno where…

WELDER JOHN. The clock is boarded up. Alright mind how you go because they just done Tescos down Well Street alright? (*Short pause*.) No I dunno where else it's spreading to but BE CAREFUL. If you get caughted up in it ya dunno what they're fucking doing do ya. Just a matter of money. See ya later. Alright. Mind how you go.

Sirens.

TURKISH SHOPKEEPER. Looka dat. Looka dat. What happened you tink, what happen there?

ALECKY. I think it's kicking off up there. I think there's / a problem.

TURKISH SHOPKEEPER. / Okay today closed. What happen tomorrow? What happen other day? Police very soft. Police should be close de road. Why traffic – still traffic working? Two van close there, two van close there, dat's it everyfing finish, nobody coming in.

ALECKY. I know, I don't know.

TURKISH SHOPKEEPER. Dis is-dis is not Turkey, dis is not U-Africa, dis is United Kingdom, democrat's country, okay dis is democrat's country, closa dis road, closa dis road, nobody coming in dat's it, clos it der… that's it finish!

ALECKY. Do you think – where do you think the fighting is now? Up there? / Where do you think?

TURKISH SHOPKEEPER. / I think somebody tell me, somebody tell me Clarence Road. Looka dat.

ALECKY. Ah, oh my God, oh my God that's pretty exciting.

Dozens of mounted police come past and head up towards the epicentre of the riot.

TURKISH SHOPKEEPER. I like, I like, I like police now. I like police, police, good good. (*Beat.*) *Good* police boy. (*Beat.*) Good police boy. (*Beat.*) Good police.

ALECKY. Phew.

She takes a photo of the horses. A man passes heading up in the direction of the horses.

TURKISH SHOPKEEPER. Okay. He going there…

ALECKY. I'm gonna look too, / thank you, bye.

TURKISH SHOPKEEPER. / Okay.

Bumping into another onlooker as she goes.

ALECKY. Ooh I'm sorry, sorry.

2. Steering Group Part A

TONY. I saw you absolutely fantastically on er on on on
Monday night standing, / we came out at midnight.

ALECKY. / Hello, hi, hi. Good to see you. Hi.

FATHER ROB. It was extraordinary.

TONY. Yeah, well it was that thing of erm… yeah no my im…
I've just been interviewed and somebody said to me if y-y-
you've got an image that you would take away… alright, it
was-it was the fact that it was coming down, uh coming out at
midnight 'n' walking down to erm… uh I hadn't been, sort of,
bold enough to sort of go outside too much… been in and out
a bit and we'd seen neighbours had things hurled at them / an'
things // 'n' so it was… it… so we sort of wandered down the
end of the road 'n' sort of saw our neighbours 'n' things like
that 'n' you were sort of like there i-in full cassock I just
thought that was, kind of, y'know… as I say – I'm not, not, ya
know I'm not a member of the church or anything but,
y'know, I just thought it was a very uh powerful image 'n'
sense of witness 'n' sort of proclamation of er-er-who you
were in a very controversial situation so yeah…

FATHER ROB. / Yeah… // yeah.

TONY. So I sort o– / respect you for that though.

FATHER ROB. / Oh thank you –

ALECKY. Amazing.

TONY. – yeah. (*Giggling*.)

FATHER ROB. It is. Eez it's quite scary standing there for
some of it all, but uh – it really was.

TONY. How l– someone said you were there nearly all night or?

FATHER ROB (*nods*). Yeah…

TONY. Wow…

FATHER ROB. I mean it stopped about three o'clock.

TONY. Yes… we peaked at two we had a sort of this car on fire
and sort of exploded out of the / front window until at about

two. // And at that point Sarah and I literally had all our
bags packed and n-the back door open ready to get out the
back door.

FATHER ROB. / Yeah… // Yeah.

ALECKY. Were you really?

TONY. Oh yeah both –

A knock at the door. SARAH *walks through to let in* ALAN
DEIN. *She can be heard in the background talking to him.*

SARAH. Come in folks. / (*To* FATHER ROB.) Hi. Thank you
for coming.

TONY. / I-I will um…

FATHER ROB. That's okay.

SARAH. Come in people.

FATHER ROB. Hi Siva!

SIVA. How are you?

FATHER ROB. I'm good. How are you?

SIVA. I'm not bad. Not bad.

FATHER ROB. Gosh, I'm so pleased you're here. That's really
good news.

SARAH. Um. Can I have a show of hands for cups of tea please?

FATHER ROB. Me, me, me.

SARAH. One, two, thr/ee.

FATHER ROB. / Me, me.

SARAH. Four. Five. / Six.

SIVA. / Everybody want.

SARAH. Does everyone want normal builders' tea?

ALL. Yeah.

ALECKY. Yes please.

SARAH. / Anyone want sugar?

ALECKY. / No thank you.

SIVA. / Yes of course I want sugar. / Can't drink without sugar.

IAN. / No thanks.

All laugh.

SARAH. One sugar?

SIVA. Yes.

TONY. Will you have herbal tea Sarah.

SARAH. Um. Siva you know everyone here.

ALAN. I'm Alan Dein, I'm from BBC Radio 4 –

IAN. Oh hi yeah.

ALAN. – and I present the series called *Lives in the Landscape*.

IAN. Yes I saw that you were gonna be doing / something yeah.

ALAN. / And-and this programme will be the first of the new series / of *Lives in the Landscape* –

IAN. / Yeah. Okay.

ALAN. – and we'll be following the situation over the next / month or so. Yeah.

IAN. / Sounds good to me. Why-why is the microphone being waved around?

Laughter.

ALAN. Because I'm going to ask who you are.

IAN. Who am I?

A knock at the door.

Erm I'm Councillor Ian Rathbone. Local councillor, that's me. A human being. There's a lot of organising to do in a situation we've you've got a lot of tension in the street and so on 'n' so… I've got some news to bring cos I've just had another meeting but uh –

ALAN. – Sounds like events are unravelling very quickly.

IAN. They are happening very very quickly yes I mean I don't know about Rob, I think Rob's basically dropped his diary this week I've dropped my diary completely this week!

FATHER ROB. It's-it's been a very hectic um week or so.

ALAN. Rob / how many meetings have you been to already? After – since Monday?

IAN. / That's all I've been doing.

FATHER ROB. Erm I mean g-gosh, quite a few. Many – most of them are chatting to people in the street – / (*His mobile rings in his pocket*.) that's the most important sort of place – Probably someone else trying to get in touch with me now – erm have to wait. (*Turns it off*.)

SARAH. / Alecky needs one… One, two, three more teas.

ALAN. I'm conscious… I'd love to talk to you… I'm conscious…

SARAH. I-I'm really sorry but we-I-it's quite amazing that we've managed to get this group of people together. / If you – if you want to chat to anyone individually can you arrange later.

IAN. / Yeah.

3. Riots Part 2

BOY 1 IN BASEBALL CAP. I know that everybody looks at us and probably thinks that we are part of it. But – (*Beat*.) can't judge a book by its cover. You never know…

A group of kids run through with scarves tied up round their faces.

They're going to where the riot is. At the top of the Narrow Way.

BOY 2 IN BASEBALL CAP. / Seems to be at Clarence Road.

BOY 1 IN BASEBALL CAP. See the / smoke in the air?

BOY 2 IN BASEBALL CAP. / There's some sorta smoke in the air.

BOY 1 IN BASEBALL CAP. Like you see, wh-oh, if you –
   when you get to this crossing if you look basically where the
   road meets, basically yeah… em… it's hard to explain but
   it's called Clarence Road 'n' that's where it's all going on. It-
   it's tense as well innit? (*Beat*.) Yeah you don't know what,
   who or what's gonna do what at any moment. (*Nervous
   giggle*.) Anyway. (*Beat*.) Take care now. See you later.

RIOTER 1. / Mo-move! Move you– Mo-move who?!

RIOTER 2. / Shut up. Shut the fuck up. What you gonna do?
   What you gonna do?

RIOTER 1. / Five-O! Five-O! Five-O wanker. Five-O, see
   five-O!

SHOCKED MAN. They're burning cars, they're looting they're
   burning, well, they went into shops 'n' they've taken shit
   outta shops.

   Showing photos from his phone.

   Well they're breaking into everything 'n' they, this place
   wasn't secured by the police before. See that shop? They
   looted everything out of it. There's people trapped in that
   house I think. This is… go from the back and you'll see it.
   And be careful.

BLING GIRL 1. If the police would sit down and listen to us
   then none of this woulda happened. Well it's their fault this
   happened in the first place. Because the whole, the whole
   thing is reflecting on that boy that got shot in the hedz,
   basically, an' if they woulda sorted that out from the
   beginning then it would've, it wouldn't of spreaded to our
   community so *we* wouldn't have to protect it and then all of
   this wouldn't of happened.

BLING GIRL 2. An' we gotta live here and we wasn't even the
   one fighting and then they mash it up but… life goes on.

   Helicopter flies overhead.

BLING GIRL 1. In this community no one's scared of any
   police officer –

BLING GIRL 2. No.

BLING GIRL 1. – cos we've approached them so many times –

BLING GIRL 2. Zactly.

BLING GIRL 1. – at the end of the day they do not scare us. They try to scare us but at the end of the day we know how to confront them 'n' we know what to say.

BLING GIRL 2. Where's the fire station round here?

ALECKY. I don't know.

BLING GIRL 1. No there's a fire.

ALECKY. Is there?

BLING GIRL 1. It's our community so we come to see what's going on.

ALECKY. And what have you seen so far?

BLING GIRL 1. Obviously nothing cos there's nothing here.

BLING GIRL 2. Earlier there was madness though.

BLING GIRL 1. Like people throwing bottles at police and then the police started throwing things back at us and then they were just raging at us and den, like… now they're setting fings on fire. (*Beat.*) Yeah.

ALECKY. So what's on fire – where – what's on – where what?…

BLING GIRL 1. This is Pembury.

ALECKY. Okay.

BLING GIRL 1. Yeah.

ALECKY. And what's on fire? A building's on fire / in there or what?

BLING GIRL 2. / Yeah buildings. Yeah.

BLING GIRL 1. Yeah. I think so. Somewhere inside the estate but I'm not sure where.

ALECKY. Right. Okay.

A helicopter swoops low overhead.

Oh my God. Did you see all the horses, I was on Mare
Street an' – ?

BLING GIRL 1. – Yeah.

BLING GIRL 2. Yeah.

BLING GIRL 1. I dunno what is the point of the horses, the
horses not – what the horses gonna do?

Beat.

ALECKY. Well I guess people on – police on a horse probably
more threatening than standing aren't they. They – it – To me
I thought 'Okay, it's kicking off now.'

BLING GIRL 1. Yeah. Cos they're fighting for what they
think's right basically.

ALECKY. But wh-what do they think's right – why – what?

BLING GIRL 1. I don't even under– I don't know.

ALECKY. Ha hhuh.

BLING GIRL 2 *laughs gently,* ALECKY *joins.*

BLING GIRL 1. I don't know, I don't know myself.

BLING GIRL 3. I'm going Angel. Cos them lot are all going
Angel.

BLING GIRL 1. Come on then.

4. Steering Group Part B

IAN. Tha– you know for me, you know, there were a lot of people just watching who shouldn't have been there –

TONY. Yeah.

IAN. – it was like a media e… for me – it was almost – certainly Mare Street – it was almost like a media event. / I-I had a slight, coupla clicks a coupla times, you know like you do think, what's reality here, is this actually sort of like actually a film thing that's going on here? You know that these are all – actors, they're not real people.

JANE. / Mhmm. Mmm.

TONY. Si-Siva. Without any irony you get the 'I Love Hackney' mug.

Laughter.

SIVA. Of course I do!

ALECKY. Thank you Sarah.

SARAH. I ha– I haven't been sleeping, I'm so wired.

TONY. Yah. / I don't any of us would have imagine ourselves at this point a week ago.

SIVA. / Definitely.

IAN. No! Certainly not! I was supposed to be decorating at my house, I haven't done single thing this week.

JANE. Yeah.

TONY (*to* SIVA). You're at the focal point of this so God knows what it's like for you. I mean you're being sent from one emotion to another.

Pause.

SARAH. Okay for e– can I just tell everyone who everyone is in case they don't know okay um…

IAN. I don't who I am. Who am I actually?

SARAH. This is Siva, everyone knows Siva.

ALECKY. Yes.

SIVA. Popular person.

SARAH. The-the famous Siva.

JANE. Local celebr– national celebrity, international-international celebrity.

Laughter.

SARAH. Uh okay um... Ian Rathbone.

IAN. Yeah I-I'm local councillor so.

JANE. I'm Jane um, I'm a local resident just up that way, um I run the market at the churchyard on a Saturday. I just went to the vigil and bumped into Sarah, was only forty-eight hours ago we worked out.

IAN. Yeah.

SARAH. By chance.

JANE. And, er, yeah. People kind of thought that we been, we were really good friends. We are really good friends now I think and us and various other people, some in New York have been erm, have basically set up this website. So – anyway so lots going on but uhm, it's all quite good.

ALECKY. Fantastic. Erm I'm Alecky Blythe and I make documentary plays so the actors kind of portray the real-/life people.

JANE. / Is there – is there a word – is there a phrase for that?

ALECKY. Verbatim.

JANE. Verbatim. Right.

ALECKY. Yep.

JANE. Brilliant, thank you.

ALAN. I'm Alan Dein uhm I present the series *Lives in a Landscape* and this is gonna be the first programme of *Lives in a Landscape* which will go out in October.

TONY. I'm Tony, I'm tea boy. Uhm, I'm also uh Sarah's husband and uh, uh, I-I run a business that does uh art direction and set building for commercials and pop videos.

SARAH. Um I'm Sarah uh I'm one of Siva's customers. I'm the person that kind of accidentally set the ball rolling uh, yeah, well – (*Beat.*) that's it really.

FATHER ROB. I'm Rob Wickam and I'm a local resident, I live on, directly on Clapton Square and I'm the rector of Hackney. Erm my traditional kind of role in all that is-is as someone who holds the curer of souls for the parish of Hackney.

Beat.

SARAH. Uhm, I've made a-a little agenda. Did you like it Ian?

IAN. Yeah that was fine.

SARAH. Do you want to…

IAN. Shall I…?

SARAH. Do you want to be the chair?

IAN. Yeah, shall I start it then? Erm… Right well the agenda according to this book – (*Holds up the very brightly coloured book with mirrored sequins on.*) ha ha, is erm. 'One. How to support er Siva.' (*Beat.*) Er sort of hold him up like this.

Laughter.

5. Riots Part 3

HINDREY ROAD MUM. People said, 'Why it started is because the guy get shoot.' It's not only that. It started Thursday of last week. Police park up right at the end of the road and they give out flyers said dey gonna raid de houses. And dey raid de houses. Dey arrested tirty-tree people, dey took tirty-tree. Outta Pembury alone dey took tirty-tree people. Dey go Tottenham, dey took a lotta dem from Tottenham and dey shot da guy. I told the police, instead you develop relationship with de people you are 'arassin' de people.

KATE. It was a sting operation and it was a sort of, it was a honey-trap thing which ya know, in America they wouldn't have been allowed to get away with it basically. There was an undercover officer living on the estate, on the Pembury for eighteen months so they sort of enticed people who they knew were kind of doing a little bit of something into ya know giving them drugs to sell and asking if they could get firearms an' all the rest of it. So, anyway it was a huge thing – ya know, it was the biggest operation they'd run for such a long time, an-blah blah blah and they were really pleased with themselves.

HINDREY ROAD MUM. What dey do is hold dem, fling dem down on da concretes – kneel dem in dere back rub dere face on da pavement. / People come out and react to that because it's not nice to see, even if it's not *your* child, to see police have dem like. *Dis* is what start da riot. (*Beat.*) Police are not surprised they know it was gonna cause disruption. Dey say war is gonna happen because of da tings dat dey are going to use young people so now dey shot da guy they make it worse. At da end of da day ev– partially all da people know dere is gonna be a riot.

ALECKY. / Mmmm. (*Beat.*) There's a story here isn't there. Yeah.

HINDREY ROAD MUM. It's sad story to see people car burning but it's not nice.

Beat. ALECKY *looks around.*

ALECKY. Gosh I'm going to go an' have a little look / but it looks a bit scary down there doesn't it? // I don't think I want to stay down there for very long.

HINDREY ROAD MUM. / Okay. // Yes. Ha ha. You have to keep on running back. Well you just have to running back and go inside again.

ALECKY. Yes. Ha!

HINDREY ROAD MUM. No one would stop you. It's alright.

ALECKY. Ha ah ah. Okay.

ALECKY *ventures into the thick of it on Clarence Road.*

RIOTER 3. Babor!

RIOTER 4. Yo.

RIOTER 3. You're not supposed to come that far innit. Come round 'ere. Babor – Babor.

A helicopter hovers overhead.

SAM. This it's basically this is, police are right at the top of this road, / just at the-where this-the-uh-the-well um bit further on from this estate. // There's a burning car there, there's a burning car just the street down there, there's a burning car street down there. (*Beat.*) I've gotta, I-I-I've manage the gardens just on a square so I just wanted to check them, that they-they're okay. Priorities, y'know I'm not worried about f– shops burning I'm worried about, y'know, lawns getting damaged.

ALECKY. / Right. // Right.

Laughter.

SAM. Yeah. I genuinely don't whether I should be here or not. / I don't know if I'm adding to the uh… chaos or not. // Just voyeurism isn't it, it's natural.

ALECKY. / He hah. // Yeah. Ha hah.

It is. It.

MAN *mutters as he passes, offering* SAM *a can of stolen beer.*

SAM. No I'm alright mate, thanks. Going into the-into the off-licence as if, as if they're not being watched but choppers up there are hundred of metres apart in-in the air are just watching people walking in 'n' out sort of uh… so uh yeah it's all a bit casual.

When you're down here you don't really think you're being filmed but there's a good chance we're on BBC News right now. Should we be here? (*Beat*). I'd be careful mate because you're on CCTV you know that? It's all on the news. (*Beat.*) It's all quite a sort of riot light isn't it. / It's like –

ALECKY. / It is.

SAM. – it's a middle-class riot. Obviously not everyone's middle class but it's, there's this, there are a few, um, gentrified people round here / or whatever so I mean poor guy whose shop that is.

ALECKY. / Yes. (*Pause.*) I might go and take a little picture on my phone and then… just like… get out of here because it is getting dark isn't it, it does feel like it's kind of at that stage of slightly… God – LOOK AT THE CAR wow that's amazing gotta get that photo. Amazing. (*Beat.*) Oh no my camera's now not working, it's typical. (*Beat.*) Oh my camera has just gone on the – that's so annoying – I can't believe it. I'm gonna turn it off and maybe turn it on again and maybe, maybe it'll work in a minute.

The violence escalates further.

Oh God.

SAM. There's a chopper right up there just filming everybody… it's kind of. There's a couple of by, bystanders, one with an Amnesty T-shirt on, which is a bit, bit of an irony… Ha.

Laughter from ALECKY *followed by a sigh from her, then a pause.*

Yeah I dunno whether this is – I'm not too sure we should be laughing / at this.

ALECKY. / I don't, no, I don't think we should be actually should we?

RIOTER 4. Be calm now, be calm now.

Looting continues in haste in the background.

RIOTER 5. Gee!

Wolf-whistles.

ALECKY. Come on phone hurry up. I wanna get my photo and get out of here.

RIOTER 6. Revolution!

Cheers and boos as looters come out of the shop laden with goods.

SAM*'s phone rings.*

SAM (*on phone*). Hello?… I'm alright thanks you alright?…
No I'm nowhere near it no… No, no I-I'm a coupla streets
off, not far away but it hasn't reached that yet… Uh… yeah a
little bit.

Sounds of the riot escalate as the shop get trashed.

Yeah… Yeah… I'm alright.

ALECKY*'s camera eventually works and she accidentally
takes a photo of the scene as a* LOOTER *loaded down with
crates of alcohol walks into shot.*

ALECKY. Oop.

LOOTER 1 (*aggressively*). Who you taking pictures of?

ALECKY. No, no, no not you.

LOOTER 1. Who you taking pictures of / me?

ALECKY. / No, no, no no.

LOOTER 1. What?

ALECKY. No, no, no, not of you.

LOOTER 1. You better not be taking no pictures of me / you
know?

ALECKY. / No.

LOOTER 1. Alright / gimme that picture then. Gimme that,
gimme right in front of me I won't take your phone, I won't
take your phone. Just gimme that picture please innit.

ALECKY. / No okay I will, I will – I will. Okay. Okay. Okay –

LOOTER 2. You can't do that, have be careful love, you can't
tek pictures.

ALECKY. – yeah of course, of course, sorry, sorry that was it,
sorry, I'll delete it.

LOOTER 1. Go to another picture.

LOOTER 2. Give her a break now man, give her a break.

ALECKY. Okay I'll go back, I'll go back. W-w-w-w-wait, here
we go, that's it.

LOOTER 1. And go next again.

ALECKY. Of the car. Okay?… Safe.

LOOTER 2. Gotta be careful.

ALECKY. Yeah. (*Pause. Then sotto voce to herself.*) So scary. (*Beat. Matter of factly.*) Right, okay, I think I might be done now here. How about you Sam?

SAM. Yeah. Yeah I think I'll come.

ALECKY. Shall we go out this way?

SAM. Yeah, why not.

6. Steering Group Part C

TONY. Well he's just the local newsagent, I mean, as in, so we don't, necessarily sort of know him socially or anything like that but he always has a, y'know, a very friendly smile and I sometimes wear sort of uh T-shirts with sort of uh, all sorts of different Indian deities on just that I got when I was sort – travelling in India and he'll always sort of comment on that or things like that so. It's-it's-it's like you're really connected to someone but it's also sort of quite impersonal as well and it's at-moments like this that it actually becomes personal and it was impossible not to feel just sort of, you know completely sort of, devastated as if we were watching, y'know, it on the news with everything being, sort of, ripped out of the building.

SARAH. You know I look at myself on the night and I reacted… from a state of fear, I was you know 'n' I sort of contracted into wanting to hide away, wanting to just stay with immediate neighbours or… I didn't feel brave enough to go out there and I felt very vulnerable you know 'n' I… I felt, and then the next day I managed to get a grip on myself and turn that around into a sort of attitude of expansiveness so operating from a completely different place, a much more positive place in myself. Y'know it-it's that polar, um, thing of fear and love, wh-which place do you operate from?

IAN. I'm answering all the media for you now you know?

SIVA. Yeah I know that…

IAN. Just bin d-dealing with *The Times*, gonna ring them back later on, but Sky News were pretty keen, on doing something so they said they've got 12.30 tomorrow so if you an' I could be around from that time tomorrow then…

FATHER ROB. I'm not free at all tomorrow.

IAN. Oh aren't you? Alright okay.

FATHER ROB. Um I-we-we-…

IAN. Well I just told them / to come to the shop and then I said I-I'd like you to meet the support group and other people and talk, talk to other people because… he's basically… exhausted. // He looks exhausted doesn't he?

FATHER ROB. / Yeah. // Yeah.

SIVA. Ahaa.

ALECKY. Yeah.

IAN *laughs*.

SARAH. See what I think is brilliant about Siva here is he is a person at the centre of a community and he knows both rich and / poor and that's why he's an important symbol and he is basically the person who is // crossing those divides already /// and we just wanna spread that out.

JANE. / Hm. // Hm. /// Hm.

SARAH. I would like to see him back to where he was have a massive community opening party / and a holiday. Holiday with the family in Sri Lanka – (*Beat*.) personally.

JANE. / Okay well that all sounds good, would you like that?

SIVA *smiles*.

Aaaaah.

SIVA. No I'm not gonna go Sri Lanka.

Laughter all round.

JANE. Or you'll go – You-You'll / go to New York. Ha ha ha ha.

IAN. / It's not a holiday.

TONY. Being a Tamil – Being a Tamil in Sri Lanka is / not easy at the moment. It's not a holiday. More of the same.

SIVA. / Yeah – I – I – i-i-… Nobody there for me.

SARAH. What are we called?

JANE. Help Siva Campaign I dunno.

IAN. Erm…

SARAH. Help Siva Campaign?

IAN. / Yeah.

JANE. / Ha ha.

SARAH. Friends of Siva?

JANE. Friends of Siva is quite nice actually.

SARAH. Friends of Siva is much better.

IAN. Friends of Siva.

SECTION 2 – Shop the Day After

7. Shop Day After

A large crowd comprising of locals and media, national and international, has gathered outside SIVA*'s looted shop to view the wreckage.* SIVA, *devastated, sits in his van parked alongside, shying way from the spotlight and waiting for the police to arrive.*

BOY ON BIKE. Hey Siva. What happen man. How come yo-you're. How come you're. How come you're on da news and that Siva man?

He reads from a note someone has stuck to the outside of SIVA*'s looted shop.*

'Dearest Siva. And Family.' Eh Siva why are you on the news though man?

SIVA *ignores. Long pause.*

Whaat's wrong?

He cycles off sneering.

LUKE. I've just been round on my bike just to check what's left of our area 'n' there's a few shops left but… obviously everyone's getting ready for tonight because the shops are boarding their windows up. O2 shop ain't even called glazers in they've just called people in to board their windows. They're getting ready for tonight. People are already saying they're coming back. Oh well I'm ready. If they come near our house I got a bat. All this G20 stuff what caused this trouble because obviously / now they have to be careful.

MALTESE MAN. / Oh yeah.

LUKE'S MUM. Yeah that was it if they had army or with watercannons.

LUKE. Before they woulda gone at 'em with batons 'n' beat the shit outta 'em 'n' they woulda shit / themselves 'n' run away.

LUKE'S MUM. / If they had nothing they can do about it. (*Beat*.) They stood down there did nuffing mate. Didn't they? They stood down there and did nuffing. The Old Bill did nuffing. They went down there, they stood there and they let them wreck the place.

MALTESE MAN. There wasn't enough police on it –

LUKE'S MUM. No they didn't do nuffing. They didn't do nuffing. They did – There was Old Bill forgot –

MALTESE MAN. They-they got 'em by, whachucallit, / by, uh, surprise.

LUKE'S MUM. / No, they didn't, no they didn't –

MALTESE MAN. Cos they moving from one place to another.

LUKE'S MUM. They didn't we were *here*. / They stood down the bottle and did nuffing. The Old Bill did nuffing. They didn't move! –

SHUTTER WOMAN. / Police are doomed if they do 'n' doomed if they don't aren't they? Catch-22. Cos if they did do something 'n' someone got hurt they'd all be out cryin'.

LUKE'S MUM. Then they run up there, then they run back down the Old Bill and disappeared, they didn't do nuffing. We were *here*. / We were there, we were there, the police didn't do nuffing. // They needed the army. ///

MALTESE MAN. / Some of the. // The police. /// Yeah of course yeah.

LUKE'S MUM. Cos all they had was a shield and a stick, / what was that against fire? Nuffing. An ambulance, couldn't get an ambulance into the estate you had to go over there – they couldn't come in cos if they would've got 'em they would've smashed them that's why.

MALTESE MAN. / Yeah.

SHUTTER WOMAN. Then why was the ambulance called here to get the kid that cut his leg that broke in the shutter?

SHOCKED MAN. See the whole stock huh? – that's the guy – it his – it's his stuff – that guy in that van.

DEANNE. He's insured yeah?

SHOCKED MAN. You gotta ask him. I don't think he's covered y'know.

DEANNE. Wh-wh-what about the in–, insurance – contents insurance. He didn't have any contents insurance?

SHOCKED MAN. Oh God. / No.

DEANNE. / Oh my God.

SHOCKED MAN. Thousands.

DEANNE. No contents insurance?

SHOCKED MAN. That's the whole stock. I'm surprised. I'm shocked. / I am cos it looks like it's-they… they've //… for thousands…

DEANNE. / Oh my God. // They made a made a mess and they didn't take it out properly. / It's true, look, definitely! It's all on the floor. // Oh my God.

SHOCKED MAN. / Mmm… // Mmm-mm.

MAN WITH CAMERA. Can I come in, take pictures?

DEANNE. Ah it's not my shop baby. It's the man in the van. You know if you wanna go 'n' in take a look then be on your own head that's what I do.

MAN WITH CAMERA. Okay I'll go.

DEANNE. Well alright then let me go first.

She enters the shop.

OLDER NORTHERN WOMAN *peers in through the shop door.*

OLDER NORTHERN WOMAN. Look at this.

She follows DEANNE *in.*

DEANNE. Just be careful cos it looks dangerous. My God, the fridges are still on. / They're still on the fridges are still on. That Irn-Bru in there must be still cold. Ah you know what I need tea you know. I do, I need tea! I'm sure he ain't gonna

mind if I ask him if I can tek a tea because I'm not a thief.
And Canderel because it's sweetener.

MAN WITH CAMERA. / Still on.

DEANNE. Oh he's being filmed I can't ask him. I don't s'pose
he'll mind now anyway.

YOUNG NORTHERN WOMAN. What's are you doing?

DEANNE. He's getting filmed innit.

YOUNG NORTHERN WOMAN. So what are you doing?

DEANNE. Getting the Canderel.

OLDER NORTHERN WOMAN *cackles*.

YOUNG NORTHERN WOMAN. What's that – are you gonna
pay him for it?

DEANNE. Yeah if he wants it.

YOUNG NORTHERN WOMAN. I think you should pay 'im
for it, you can't st-keep looting.

DEANNE. Who's looting / who's looting?

OLDER NORTHERN WOMAN (*laughing*). / Did I pay for it?

YOUNG NORTHERN WOMAN. What are you doing?

OLDER NORTHERN WOMAN. / At least you don't have to go
Tescos now love.

DEANNE. / They pinched the tea. I can't see the tea.

YOUNG NORTHERN WOMAN. What you gonna take that
are you?

DEANNE. No I'm gonna ask him for it.

YOUNG NORTHERN WOMAN. And what you gonna do, just
see if you can take it?

DEANNE. If he wants mo-money he can get money obviously.
Cos I'm not a looter. But he doesn't have PGs, so it'll have
to be Tetley, lemme see if he want money for it.

SHOCKED MAN *laughs*.

She exits the shop.

She goes over to SIVA *in his van.*

Here sweetheart – (*Knocking abruptly on the window.*) here's some money, here. I want to buy this from you. Here, don-don't panic yeah? Don't panic. Lemme see what change I have in here. None. (*Laughs.*) I have to go to the whaducallit. To the bank. Here see two pound here. It's alright go on, tek it, tek it. Here heh? You've still got stuff in there to sell. Alright?

OLDER NORTHERN WOMAN. Good for you gal.

DEANNE. Yeah might as well innit? / Well it's the first start innit.

OLDER NORTHERN WOMAN. / Help-'elp toward it.

DEANNE. It's not all of us did this you know?

OLDER NORTHERN WOMAN. No. He's such a lovely guy, eh?

SIVA. Many a lovely guy this has happen to you.

OLDER NORTHERN WOMAN. I know darling.

SIVA. When-when it's all of this when you're good this'll happen to you.

OLDER NORTHERN WOMAN. Isn't it? He's such a lovely guy I tell ya everybody talks about this man on the street.

ALECKY. I'm so sorry. I'm so sorry. What-what-what happens now? What-what-what do you do now?

SIVA. Dunno.

PLAIN-CLOTHES POLICEMAN. Guys can we just ask – this is a crime scene at the moment, can we ask if you just move back so we can get the scenes of crimes officers through please?

AMERICAN JOURNALIST. Can you step back a little a bit?

ALECKY. Yeah sure.

AMERICAN JOURNALIST. Lovely thanks.

ALECKY. Right sorry.

AMERICAN JOURNALIST. Cos you're a writer aren't you?

ALECKY. Yes, yeah / I'm not... yeah.

AMERICAN JOURNALIST. / No – Yes... okay... sort of.

PLAIN-CLOTHES POLICEMAN. Have you had the scenes of crimes officers down yet?

SIVA. Not yet I'm just waiting for it.

PLAIN-CLOTHES POLICEMAN. They're on their way they're just... down the road.

SIVA. Okay.

PLAIN-CLOTHES POLICEMAN. Erm... what exactly – has-has anyone got in?

SIVA. No. Just completely broken away, just put the shutter back.

PLAIN-CLOTHES POLICEMAN. You put the shutter back down?

SIVA. Just now yeah.

OLDER NORTHERN WOMAN. Sad. My heart bleeds for him.

ALECKY (*to* SIVA). Can I-can I talk to you?

AMERICAN JOURNALIST. Do you mind waiting / a second do you mind?...

ALECKY. / Oh sorry sorry sorry.

AMERICAN JOURNALIST. Thank you.

HEIDI. Hiya, 'allo my name's Heidi, I'm from the *Hackney Herald*. I'm really sorry about what happened, can I give you my card first of all just so you've got it. How – can I ask how long you've owned the shop?

SIVA. Eleven years.

HEIDI. Eleven years? God, how did you hear what happened?

SIVA. Seen the Sky.

HEIDI. You seen it – you saw it on the news? / Oh my God. 'N' so what did you think, did you come down?

SIVA. / News yeah. But I couldn't get through, police didn't let me to come in.

HEIDI. Right. God. That must ha' been awful.

ALECKY. Maybe the community can do something y'know maybe, maybe they / can do something.

OLDER NORTHERN WOMAN. / Try and get 'em to help.

SIVA. You just never thought you'd have to, never happen to you, it-it's to say wh-when you-you live in London you never thought these kind of riots come to you.

SECTION 3 – Gets Active

8. Steering Group Part D

TONY. I mean we were sort of sitting in the bath 'n' just sort of wondering about y'know wh-what we could do, in terms of, um doing something to help. Uh I think, what happened first, was you… / we ca–…

SARAH. / I-I-I started by hassling erm our local councillors and saying what are you gonna do? You know is anyone supporting Siva and the other local businesses? And my local councillor wrote back and said, 'why don't you do something?' Threw it back to us and, uh, / we just thought it would be great to set up a fund.

TONY. / An' we –

We just originally just went and got sort of, uh, helped Siva at hotmail.co.uk.

SARAH. No. FundforSiva.

TONY. Oh it was FundforSiva at that point. / Gosh I've even forgot yeah no –

SARAH. / hotmail.co.uk

TONY. – It's all moving so fast-hh. And then from that then sort of knew someone who – in America who actually sort of built the website over the day 'n'…

SARAH. When the web designer went to bed last night in New York the tally was already about five thousand pounds.

TONY. In under twelve hours… y'know it really is… working which is quite amazing. We're making this up as we go along this was sort of like made up in the middle of the night – I mean literally we've, sort of sending a note to a friend who we know from Burning Man uh, used to organising community, and literally just thought, sent an email last night saying y'know: 'roses are red, violets are blue, we're helping

Siva and you're in the crew' and that's it, y'know, it's kinda
like, it's not exactly democracy in action.

IAN. / Okay. Can we do – we're gonna try and move us on. //

JANE. / So – so sorry.

SARAH. Okay who's / going to write a –

    // Okay.

JANE. J– But sorry just to go back to these, / so in terms of the,
y'know *This Morning* and whoever else, are we, we're just
saying-we're saying no to those are we?

    Pause.

SIVA. Yesssss.

IAN. You, so you *don't* want to do *This Morning*?

SIVA (*very quietly*). No.

JANE. You go into a studio, and you be interviewed in a studio,
it's like a-a studio / int–

IAN. / Yeah see it's interesting. I think-I think we should do
that. / But I think generally we keep –

JANE. / I think we probably should.

SARAH. Wh-hang on hang on I think Siva ought to make the
decision / I mean it's not an easy thing to do without any // –

TONY. / Yeah. // I've done live TV. It was quite a big stress for
me.

    Beat.

FATHER ROB. Right, um, / in terms of the party itself now I
don't know whether this will be enough, just never know these
things, the tea party itself is being sponsored by Marks and
Spencer's. // Marks and Spencer's ha– are putting the
resources in to create a tea party for up to four hundred people.

IAN. / Yes.

ALECKY. // Mmm.

JANE. Great.

ALECKY. Wow.

TONY. Okay so they-re-they're doing all of that?

FATHER ROB. They're doing all of that. I mean I spoke to
their directors today, it's gone to a really high level. Marks
and Spencer's got the idea from their-their perspective is if-if
it works well 'n' they're doing little bags for children, little
bags of sweets for children –

ALECKY. Mmmmm.

JANE. Oh excellent.

IAN. Fantastic.

FATHER ROB. – bananas and bunting and tablecloths 'n' /
plates 'n' cups.

JANE. / Oh excellent.

SARAH. Oh brilliant.

FATHER ROB. – they're doing the whole works –

JANE. Wow.

FATHER ROB. – Erm with the idea that if-if it works well then
they'll roll it out to, for-for all the other stores to do who have
been in areas which have been affected by riots / so I think for,
I mean, y'know // it's-it's an impressive piece of work.

JANE. / Oh well that's quite good.

IAN. // That's a nice story isn't it Jane?

TONY. Has anyone looked what the weather might be?

ALECKY. Mmmm.

SARAH. It was sunny intervals last night perhaps you could
pray for that?

JANE. Mmm.

SIVA. Yeah. Ha ha ha.

JANE. Um I'm really sorry to – I know I keep harking on about this but I think it's really important 'n' I and… I've just got an email from the woman from *This Morning*. You've just been on the-on the news / and my husband said it's really, it's really powerful and it's gonna, it's, I hate to kinda land this on your shoulders I know what you've been through but it's-it's what can be raised for other people and I mean they-they're saying they'd love to have you on *This*, on *This Morning* and they'll talk about the website and they'll-they'll promote it 'n' they'll talk about it in a-in a wider, wider issue so maybe // that's just something –

IAN. / Yeah I just got it too –

FATHER ROB. // Jane? Are you free on Monday morning?

Beat.

JANE. Yeah.

FATHER ROB. Can you go with – I mean if Siva was happy with this can you go with him –

JANE. Yeah I mean –

FATHER ROB. – and sit next to him in the studio and –

JANE. Or – or Sarah.

SARAH. Yeah could-we could all come.

FATHER ROB. – or Sarah or whoever.

JANE. Everybody I mean I-uh-I-uh I mean you don't have to answer / now I just I think –

SIVA. / Nah if-if-if…

JANE. – this isn't just about you without being / putting it…

SIVA. / Right if-if-if it's will – ya know-good cause / ya know – followed by – people might – ya know need it y'know? //

JANE. / It's Eamonn – // 'n' we can steer it. It'll be less about you now in a way / and more about what y-you can, we can steer it that way and you can talk a bit more about the wider community so it'll be less focused on you and your // trauma.

SIVA. / It's true.

IAN. // Can we-can we insist then…?

SARAH. Does he even want to go at all I think is / the question first // and I think it needs thinking about.

TONY. / Yeah. No I think…

SIVA. // A lot of things you have to do it you know just every, y'know every single day I wa' asked 'What you feel…' Just…

JANE. You find it quite st– do you find it quite stressful?

SIVA. Ye-yeah.

JANE. Yeah that's understandable, yeah. But I just wondered, I mean y-y-of course you have to say what you-how you feel but I just wondered if it would make it any easier if it was a diff-managed a bit differently and we did it very short-term 'n' 'n'…

SIVA. The reason is everybody asking the same question, they say, 'Is the people, did the local people who dunnit?'/ Everybody ask the same question, 'Do you think local people done it?'// I'm gonna serve them again. What can I say?

IAN. / Yeah.

JANE. // Ahh.

Beat.

IAN. Yeah.

SECTION 4 – Mash-Up Debate at the Public Meeting

9. We Know Who Dunnit

STEVE. And we act-we actually know who the people are that actually robbed that poor man's shop there. We *know* who dunnit, right? I've got witnesses that will swear anything that who dunnit and it hasn't been done yet and it will be done 'n' people from off this estate was doing that and they was singing and dancing up the end of the road there and you know why people don't say anything? Because they're afraid that som'ink gonna come through their front-room window...

DOT. Where's their parents? They couldn't 'ave bin more than ten-ten year old.

STEVE. And that's the tenants – that's the tenants that live on this estate. / An' I see 'em. An' I, I actually see 'em.

DOT. / Yes.

10. Popped the Lock

KYLE. Like, did I tell you what happen yeah? No locals did that, innit? No locals popped the lock, innit? Let me d– Like one of my people opposite Siva's place said he saw some white guy pop the shutters. I'm not being funny, not being racist, black people don't know how to pop shutters innit, they're more on the dealing side of things innit. Like I'm-I'm not gonna lie innit, the white guy popped the-popped the lock, got the big bag of goodies, brung it out 'n' said, 'This is for you lot.'

11. Not That Smart

DEANNE. This was not set up by any criminal gangs – we ain't got gangs smart enough. All the gangs round h-here allegedly smoke weed and sleep all day. How the hell they gonna set up – how the hell they gonna set up flippin' riots across the country? You understand? They're not that smart! (*Beat.*) No! If they were smart then they would have robbed some of the banks them then innit?!

12. Mini Revolution

COLIN. No but dey say where – da people was looting wasn't from this area though. I was here cos I was guarding my shop all through it. It was all strangers. Obviously there was some people from de area but da majority was w-w-hehe-w-hehe-w-w-area – ya know what I mean?... The locals wouldn't break into the shop but he-he de the locals went into it when it was broken he-he.

SEVEN-POUND CLIENT. How much do you charge for a haircut?

COLIN. Seven pounds.

SEVEN-POUND CLIENT. Okay well I have my one done.

COLIN. Okay take a seat. (*Beat.*) But it's a revolution innit. It's a mini relev-revolution it's a young people's revolution 'n' eh all revolutions have lootings y'know. (*Chuckle.*) All revolutions has fire. So this is kinda a mini rele-revolution. Yes... This is a little revolution and it hasn't stopped here yet. When you see kids throwing bricks and den dey sending messages 'It was the best day of my life,' 'n' you know what musta came off their chest? The first time they probably started a young age that they've actually stood up for something. They haven't had chance, the first time they had been able to express themselves to a bigger – audience.

Pause. Sound of snipping hair.

It was like war wasn't it?

13. Parallel Universe

REEVES CORNER WOMAN 2. Them them youngsters like to get their views across you see? 'N' they're saying, like, 'aw there's nothing to do'–

REEVES CORNER WOMAN 1. Well that's no excuse. / For doing that.

REEVES CORNER WOMAN 2. / There's nothing to do. You know, I said well I said, surely they can fi– they can go and find some– / something to do.

REEVES CORNER WOMAN 1. / 'N' I think over the years we have excused far too much – behaviour. 'N' I hear it every day professionally. F– / I'm, sick of it. And my husband's a deputy head and he hears it. Sick of it. Whatever the situation, you cannot ever, in my opinion, // justify this – what we've had over London in the last, what, four or five nights.

REEVES CORNER WOMAN 2. / Nothin' to do… // –ify. What we've had, I've seen it, my God.

REEVES CORNER WOMAN 1. I think there is a real divide in this country that is vast. It's a parallel universe that we are living in, and I'm sure you'd agree with that, it's a parallel universe. / Of the workers and the ones that don't.

REEVES CORNER WOMAN 2. / –llel universe.

REEVES CORNER WOMAN 1. There's a whole culture that-that / they are… they-they-they're meshed in this culture of-of – // of hand-me-down isn't it?

REEVES CORNER WOMAN 2. / Culture that, it's their culture. // An' they don't work, the mothers-the mothers never work, the kids never work, they go on unemployment.

REEVES CORNER WOMAN 1. Give me / give me –

REEVES CORNER WOMAN 2. / Give me give me – I want this I want that.

REEVES CORNER WOMAN 1. – and because – they've got no val– I really do believe that / – because there's no value in anything they don't care.

REEVES CORNER WOMAN 2. / Yeah.

REEVES CORNER WOMAN 2. I think it's shocking.

14. Collateral Damage

KATE. There was nothing other up there than anti-police going on. Really not. Above Siva's shop, there was nothing to do with looting, pillaging, nicking, robbing – They were not out to damage their own community at all, they weren't, I know a few wheelie bins were set on fire but you know that was collateral damage as they say. It is insulting to young people who had real political sort of reasons for being involved as in the way they conceive themselves in society, the-the way they feel the police treat them, the *constant* sort of you know jibing and picking at them they're such tossers yeah, so you can see how it erupted up there. (*Beat*.) My son comes out of his house 'n' he's stopped and searched just because he happens to be there, he's mixed-race and he happens to be there. On the day of the riot twice in five minutes he was stopped and searched, he was *manhandled*, he was mauled by one officer. (*Beat*.) Race is a hundred per cent a part of it. Because the police are inherently racist, but the stop 'n' search thing, has been *so* intolerable you can understand why they all hate them. They *hate* them.

15. Moulded

KYLE. We just don't like the police innit, they've been moulding us for too long innit, when we was kids they used to break the law innit of like bring it back – (*Pause*.) They used to do funny stuff innit they used to offer us out for fights they use to – they use to search us like ten times in one day. So they forced bare with our hands innit to think this way and to-to deal with this innit so obviously that's where the hate comes from originally. Like anyway I was just blaming the police innit, they moulded into what the guy I am.

16. Section 60

JEROME. Erm a few months ago the police locked this whole area down, they called it a Section 60.

TYRONE. Yeah.

JEROME. Yeah. I dunno what that means / yeah.

TYRONE. / Means they stop 'n' search / anybody.

JEROME. / Stop 'n' search anyone and that's exactly it I was over de over side of da road yeah? / I've come over to see what's happening, the geezer's grabbed me, thrown me up the car, searched me, done my name-check 'n' everyfink, as he's writing out my form he's saying I'm a female, he's saying I'm Chinese – yeah.

TYRONE *laughs*.

On my stop 'n' search form, proper tak– proper taking the piss out of me – //

TYRONE. / Yeah. // Yeah.

JEROME. – 'n' then after that we've had a little – a little discussion, an argument, / geezer is *squeezing* me by my throat, I couldn't breathe, they can do what they want, they are the da authority, they can do whatever dey want. // I felt like –

TYRONE. / Ya see – serious! See. // You see-you see this brings up-brings up anger within people cos like I said I know… I know a lot of people that's…

JEROME. I've had my pride – yeah – I felt-I felt like I've had my pride ripped outta me then-that day 'n' ever since I've I've had a different view to the police.

17. Can't Be Bovered

STEVE. Right I'm the chairman of the Tenants' Association on the estate.

DOT. Steve's tryna do all these things and they're not really interested.

STEVE (*breathy*). No. Y'see that-that-that there are some, there are some bad ones on here / y'know what I mean? With our youth club that we've got. The most they ever get in the youth club is about twenty, twenty-four, say top whack thirty, thirty youths 'n' how many youths must we have on this estate? You've gotta have – woah – three, four, five hundred? Six hundred?

DOT. / There is.

I think, if you want the honest truth, I think people know about it but the parents can't be bovered. All they do is chuck their children out in the street 'n' I think, and that is you'll find, that is why you don't get a lotta the kids there because they're just left to play 'n' they're told to play on the estate 'n' nowhere else.

18. Nothing to Do

TYRONE. All dese kids are *a*ngry because there is no money out here, there's nuffing for them to do, like y'get me? Sooo, there's no youth centres, y'get me, there's nu-nuffing for them to, really, y'know teach them, bring dem out of – half of dese kids probably dey ain't even been out of Hackney.

19. Outings

DOT. No that's their excuse.

STEVE. That's their / excuse.

DOT. / That's their excuse.

STEVE. I think it was just for…

DOT. That's their excuse sayin' it's boredom 'n' everything but there is a youth club here.

STEVE. Yeah, there is a youth club. There's plenty of things that can do, we run trips from here for holidays, if you're in the holidays, we do different trips where – it's just down to the parents whether they wanna take 'em on the trips. And I think you'll find a lotta the parents haven't got time I don't think. / They don't 'ave time to take 'em.

DOT. / No. We went to Clacton. We jus– last week we went to Clacton. / We're going to the // zoo in a coupla weeks' time.

STEVE. / Yeah. // We bin to err… But there's plenty of things that we do an' just put – people don't put their names down or – (*Beat.*) anything like that y'know what I mean?

20. My Name is Sadie

SADIE. Hi, um, my name is Sadie, um, I'm a resident on Pembury estate. Um I wonder if there's anyone else here from Pembury estate?

MAN AT MEETING. Yes.

SADIE. On the estate itself is bin a dispersal zone for more than five years which means that kids, they are not allowed to go out and stand around in what is *their* social space because there is no spaces in the flats. People are living in their… li– sleeping in their living rooms as bedrooms because they're overcrowded. They are not allowed to move in more than groups of two otherwise they'll get split up. Now if you're a middle-class kid in Islington, y'know, you can go out, you can drink, you can smoke… pot whatever teenage kids want

to do but if you live on Pembury estate you're gonna get
arrested for just standing out in the street talking. Um, the
youth service has been cut massively. EMA's been cut and
it's no wonder the riots happened. It was the – it was the,
y'know, it was a cry of pain that's what it was. So we need a
campaign that stops these young people being, overly, um,
prosecuted and ruin their future and also to look at the
underlying causes of what's happened.

Applause.

21. Let's Meet Again

KATE. Hi, I live on Pembury.

SADIE. Oh hiya.

KATE. Yes, an' we've got-I've got lots and lots of sort stuff
about all this. I mean my son's been arrested for violent
disorder ya know and I've got four years of history of him
being half-killed by the police, y'know et cetera et cetera.
(*Beat.*) I'm surprised I don't know you actually.

SADIE. Yeah.

KATE. Um so there's just the most extraordinary shit happening
/ y'know re: the estate but also the young people. (*Beat.*) I
mean they-they've scoured most of those young people off
that estate now as I'm sure you know, but they *did* // two
weeks before the riots.

SADIE. / Yeah. // Yeah.

KATE. And the riots seemed to have suited the police so
amazingly well. / D'you know what I mean? (*Beat.*) Because
they've now managed to come in and as-as y'know, it's been
said in the press, blanket arrest. All these people and-and
y'know digging for evidence afterwards and it's absolutely
shocking. // Don't you think?

SADIE. / Yeah. // We need to y'know –

KATE. So I –

SADIE. – we-we're parents – mums on the Pembury, we need to um start a parents' campaign or a campaign / for all kids like now –… Yeah.

KATE. / We definitely do because right now, up until now there hasn't been a voice. I was speaking to a woman who writes articles for the *Guardian*, y'know she said is there another voice? For this? 'N' I said no not really it's all kind of fragmented and people are / y'know, people aren't really interested – I think we should –

SADIE. / Well let's start having regular, let's start, let's get together the three of us / and pull other people in –

KATE. Yeah definitely.

SADIE. – Gimme your uh, your contact details.

KATE. Yes.

Beat.

ALECKY. Do you know about um, the reason I know about it is because I've been spending um quite a bit of time up-up on Clarence Road –

SADIE. Yeah.

ALECKY. – um and there's gonna be um, there's a meeting and they're having a tea party? / About erm –

SADIE. / Who is?

ALECKY. We-it's being run by the Clapton Square Users Group but it is for the Pembury – / it's with Steve Lord.

KATE. / No way.

SADIE. Well he's with / Steve Lord is the chair – well he's… yeah… but…

KATE. / Haven't been informed though have we?

ALECKY. No but he-they they're going to come round 'n' they're going to leaflet you.

KATE. Oh are they, oh okay.

SADIE. But how interesting –

ALECKY. Is this the sorta thing you might want to –

SADIE. Well we will but it's very interesting isn't it that um –

KATE. Yeah. I'm not interested in that.

SADIE. No I'm not interested in it either.

KATE. Clapton Square / is such // a far-off cry from Pembury estate /// it really is –

ALECKY. / Why?

SADIE. // Yeah... Clapton-Clapton Square –

ALECKY. /// Yeah. I know that.

KATE. – it really is. They don't have the issues / y'know the issues are not relevant.

SADIE. / But why do Clapton Square want to have a meeting, organise a meeting for Pembury estate?

ALECKY. No for listen – I got it wrong?

KATE. A tea party? It should be *on* the estate don't you think? / I know. I know, I know. I know 'n' actually, wave goodbye –

SADIE. / It's the same people with the brooms / who came down to sweep up symbolically and wave brooms around – and the Save Siva campaign. We all know Siva we love Siva but-but sorry, y'know, he-he // got caught up in the wake.

KATE. / – No I know we do. // And that sweep-up campaign was to wave bye-bye –

SADIE. Yes.

KATE. – to all those young boys.

SADIE. Yeah.

KATE. – that had been carted away.

SADIE. Yes.

KATE. – and are on remand in prison / but, y'know, I don't see too many people from Clapton Square on remand.

SADIE. / Yeah.

No.

KATE. D'you know what I mean?

SADIE. No. (*Beat.*) The three of us should meet, pretty / soon.

KATE. / Definitely, yeah definitely.

SADIE. Yeah.

KATE. And it's nothing to do with Clapton Square. (*Beat.*) I mean y'know some people talk about it and some people live it. We actually live it.

SECTION 5 – Tea Party Preparations and Stop Criminalising Hackney Youth

22. Heavy-handed

IAN. Hi there. Do you – Have you heard about the Siva campaign?

He's really getting that shop together.

JANE. Hi. How's it going?

MAN WITH DONATION. I've gotta fiver if you accept money do you?

JANE. Yes we've got – you know what we've just had our donation box taken away / but –

MAN WITH DONATION. / Not stolen? (*Laughs.*)

JANE. Not stolen no, it's happened to me, that's happened to me before. We have been watching but thank you very much that's really kind of you.

MAN WITH DONATION. Okay? Thank you.

JANE. That's great.

IAN. I tell you what the-the police are, really, y'know, I know that – y'know they probably got a tip-off or something 'n' they're, but they're really heavy-handed. I mean they've just come 'n' they –

JANE. Someone told me else…

IAN. – There was about *eight* standing there on Orchard Grove there y'know where it runs into Clarence Road 'n' there were four others patrolling 'n' just in the last, two vanloads passed me by. Ya know. Yeah. And –

JANE. I saw police cars with sirens just squeezing / down Clarence Road.

IAN. / Yeah. And-and also, if they do have a heavy presence, some people feel insulted like y'know I'm having my event 'n' there's all these cops round here do they think we're troublemakers y'know? / We know how to run our event – being a bit neurotic – but it's worrying me that we don't get a large number of them so I'm gonna ring up the cops today to say // please don't, hanging around y'know just –

JANE. / Yeah. // Large number of them, the police? Can you tell the police what to do? / Are you that powerful?

IAN. – / well nooo.

JANE. Excellent.

IAN. I'm afraid not but I can advise them can't I?

23. Stop and Search

GIRL ONLOOKER 1. What's going on there?

ALECKY *walks on to where the police are talking to a black teenager on his bike.*

BOY ONLOOKER 1. Now shut up man dat's my boy's big bruva.

ALECKY. Do you know what's going on? Do you know what's going on? I'm writing a play, I'm doing research I'm just wondering if you know what's going on? (*Pause.*) No? Do you know what's going on?

GIRL ONLOOKER 2. The police are just trying to harass the little kids.

BOY ONLOOKER 2 *shushes her.*

Dat's all.

BOY ONLOOKER 1. Just be cool yeah man.

BOY ONLOOKER 2. What's she doin'?

ALECKY. I make plays.

BOY ONLOOKER 1. Can you turn that off?

ALECKY. Okay.

Long silence as ALECKY *goes over to the police who are searching the boy and starts talking to another onlooker, without her Dictaphone turned on. We see the action play out but hear nothing.*

So tell me, tell me what happened again I don't I had the volume on. Oh God…

MAN ONLOOKER 1. You didn't have the volume / on?

ALECKY. No. Tell me / again.

MAN ONLOOKER 1. Oh dat is very unprofessional / *very* unprofessional.

ALECKY. / Tell me again. I know tell me again.

MAN ONLOOKER 1 (*chuckles*). Well listen I was standing over there / yeah?

ALECKY. / Yeah.

MAN ONLOOKER 1. 'N' all I saw was these two police bike drove down 'n' they came here, stopped here, selected one yout and just started to talk to 'im. You cannot just select, a yout 'n' just take him offa da street just like dat 'n' just start to harass him. Dat is not right, dat is *inti*midation.

MAN ONLOOKER 2. Uh? Is he under arrest?

PC1. No!

MAN ONLOOKER 2. Is he free to go?

PC 3. Sir, put your bag down there.

PC1. He just… / I've gotta search him for drugs down 'ere.

MAN ONLOOKER 2. / Is he under arrest? Is he free to go?

PC1. To be honest mate, he's very –

MAN ONLOOKER 2. Do you have a warrant?

PC1. I'm talking to him you're actually not making things any easier for me.

MAN ONLOOKER 2. Okay who-who's the officer, who's the sergeant out here?

PC1. I am. In charge.

MAN ONLOOKER 2. Okay.

PC2. He'll be finished in about one minute sir.

MAN ONLOOKER 2. Alright, sixty seconds it is.

PC1. Tell him to chill out. You're not having any problems are you?

BOY ON BIKE. It's alright, it's – don't worry.

MAN ONLOOKER 2. You sure?

MAN ONLOOKER 1. Don't be silly –

MAN ONLOOKER 2. – it's bordering harassment you're on de camera.

MAN ONLOOKER 1. – don't listen to what he says bruv, don't listen – don't be – don't programme – don't make dem programme you my brudda. Dat's why it's good to read you kna– / 'n' know your rights 'n' all.

BOY BEING SEARCHED. / But the longer you talk, the longer gotta stand 'ere innit.

PC1. See the thing is I can't actually do what I wanna do with him / because you're getting involved.

MAN ONLOOKER 1. / Yes you could.

MAN ONLOOKER 2. What are you try/na do wiv him? – // get his name and number 'n' wiv what?

MAN ONLOOKER 1. / You could. You could.

PC2. // He's tryna do a name-check.

PC1. I-I need to do a name-check, it's none of your business.

PC2. He's tryna do a name-check, he won't talk to me.

MAN ONLOOKER 2. I'm not arguing here, one second sir, listen / one person speak at a time – right forget about it.

PC2. / No, no listen he's tryna-he's tryna deal wiv this, the sooner he deals wiv it he can go. When he's talking to you / he can't do that can he?

MAN ONLOOKER 1. / So what did… what did he do? What did *he* do?

PC2. We've had some information.

MAN ONLOOKER 1. On him?

PC2. That-that he *may*, *may*…

MAN ONLOOKER 1. May?

MAN ONLOOKER 2. / May?

PC2. / May.

MAN ONLOOKER 2. It's a sticky word.

MAN ONLOOKER 1. May?

PC2. – be involved in some drugs. / We're doing our checks.

MAN ONLOOKER 1. / You're using that word may?

How can you / use the word, officer?

PC2. / Wha-wha-what we do, what we do –

MAN ONLOOKER 1. Officer? Officer? How can / you use –

PC2. / The word we'd use is investigation. Investigation. That's what we do. Give us a chance to do it and everyone goes home happy yeah?

MAN ONLOOKER 2. / Where you going?

PC1. Hey, hey, / hey!

MAN ONLOOKER 3. Where you go?

MAN ONLOOKER 2. This is out of order.

PC1. He doesn't wanna talk to you that's why he's asked us to go round there. He doesn't want to talk to you.

He asked the officer to go round there to get away from you.

MAN ONLOOKER 2. Is that what he said?

PC1. That's what he said.

MAN ONLOOKER 1. Then what you do. If you, If you… If you're talkin' about drugs then put him in the van and search him properly or take him down to the station. What you're doing is illegal.

PC2. Have you – Are you a police officer?

MAN ONLOOKER 1. I read, my brother. I study history.

And I study the law.

PC2. Just trying to do our job, yeah?

MAN ONLOOKER 1. Now is it… Now I'm asking you a question as an officer; is it right for him to search him right there, sah…

PC2. It is.

MAN ONLOOKER 1. Why don't they take him in the van?

MAN ONLOOKER 2. Whoo… Is that the truth?

PC1. That's the truth.

MAN ONLOOKER 2. Where's your warrant card. May I have a look at it.

PC1. Don't need to see my warrant card. / I'm in full uniform my friend. //

MAN ONLOOKER 2. / Why not? // No you're not.

PC1. Course I am.

MAN ONLOOKER 2. I can buy that biker's coat at a, at a shop. / I can buy a helmet.

PC1. / There's a little bit of a clue there. Little bit of a clue.

MAN ONLOOKER 2. What does that mean. You telling me I can't stick – stickers / on my my my coat.

PC1. / Nah, it'll be illegal.

MAN ONLOOKER 3. Give it up. Let him have his day off.

PC1. Eh, what bike have you got?

MAN ONLOOKER 2. What bike do I have?

PC1. Yeah.

MAN ONLOOKER 2. What you asking questions for man. I don't understand.

PC2. Because we asked him, it's down to him where he wishes to be searched. He's happy enough for it to be done in public so it's not an issue is it? (*Beat*.) We're not / gon–

MAN ONLOOKER 1. / Oh, he wanted it to be done in public?

PC2. We will naturally do things in public but if he, if he wanted it to be done in somewhere more private then that would be an issue.

MAN ONLOOKER 1. But I thought… okay… So I… let me, let me ask one more question… no…

just a silly question

Now, if *you* as an officer –

PC2. Hm-m.

MAN ONLOOKER 1. – find something on him –

PC2. Yeah?

MAN ONLOOKER 1. – and you take him to the police station –

PC2. Yes sir.

MAN ONLOOKER 1. – and the desk sergeant –

PC2. Yes.

PC1. Well you said you'd put a sticker on your bike.

MAN ONLOOKER 2. No I'm not gonna stick a sticker on my bike. Come on now, I mean, what's to say you're a police officer? There's nothing to say that.

PC1. See it on the back?

MAN ONLOOKER 2. Is it.

Mate, you ain't got no ID on you.

You're hiding your identification. Why?

PC1. What's that.

MAN ONLOOKER 2. That gives us nothing.

PC1. It's right there.

MAN ONLOOKER 2. That gives us nothing.

PC1. How am I / hiding?

MAN ONLOOKER 2. / Constable Way, Constable Sweet-Talk.

PC1. How am I hiding? (*Beat*.) Well it can't be any clearly printed than it is. (*Beat*.) That's who I am.

MAN ONLOOKER 1. – would the desk sergeant make you search him again?

PC2. It depends what it is that was found on him sir.

MAN ONLOOKER 1. Y-you see I *know* the desk sergeant would make you search him again because –

PC2. Well it depends to what extent you mean / whenever anybody goes into custody their item – because it's all on camera, audio and visual, it's, somebody is always searched again. If someone's found, say with a weapon or drugs on them they're often strip-searched as well to make sure nothing is hidden intimately.

MAN ONLOOKER 2. Who is that? That's a number.

PC1. I'm sure a man of your intelligence can work out I'm not hiding that I have any identification. I've asked you. You haven't got any identification on display have you? (*Beat*.) You've got that much on display.

MAN ONLOOKER 2. I'm not pretending to be a police officer am I?

PC1. You're pretending to know what you're talking about (*Laughs*.)

MAN ONLOOKER 2 . / No.

PC2. Cos I'm not saying he's guilty or anyfing.

MAN ONLOOKER 2. Good day Mister Microphone? Can we cross the road I don't like this / camera.

ALECKY. / Why?

MAN ONLOOKER 1. See you being there was good.

ALECKY. Yeah.

MAN ONLOOKER 1. Because if you wasn't there or we wasn't there they woulda handled him shabbier.

MAN ONLOOKER 2. If you weren't there they woulda definitely tried something / silly?

MAN ONLOOKER 1. / Yeah.

ALECKY. Really?

MAN ONLOOKER 2. It was that device that more or less
saved us. I'm telling / you da truth.

ALECKY. / Really?

MAN ONLOOKER 1. / Yeah

Is that camera still facing us?

ALECKY. Oh I see. Oh I see. It's over there now.

MAN ONLOOKER 2. Okay.

24. Wild West

KATE. It was-it was like the bloody wild west and they had a big
sort of, you know, portfolio with all these people's faces in.
Do you recognise any of these 'n' I said. 'How *dare* you come
and start asking people, to, identify? Y'know what are you
doing?' 'Oh don't you want to see the criminals arrested?' I
said no I don't. I said you've got no evidence right now,
you've got no proof any of these people did anything. At all.
Let me tell you they were smashing people's doors off, my son
was arrested. He was at the bottom of Clarence Road kicking a
ball around with two other boys and this guy in a mobility –
on a mobility cart went up and said to the police 'That – They
were involved in the riots,' and it seems to me that was
enough. He was in – he was kept in – he was, taken to
Hackney Police Station, kept in custody overnight, rushed
through to Westminster Magistrate's Court. The next day: put
in front of a judge and remanded. *No* evidence what-so-ever.

25. Leaflet Arrives

SADIE. Ya know what will we have now but a load of young people coming out of prison with drug addictions an' criminal records an' er in – being exposed to other hardened criminals. An' ya know, it's jus' gonna make the area worse. Yeah – so last week there was about ten of us I think and that was the very first meeting – we just have to build something now. I think just have a very clear, sure-footed campaign that aims to uhm protect those young people that have bee– or defend those young people that have been arrested so that they're not scapegoats cos yes ya know, they have uhm committed crimes but they shouldn't be disproportionally punished.

ALECKY. Brilliant Sadie thank you so much for / talking to me so much that's great. // Uhm…

SADIE. / Okay, no worries. // Junk.

ALECKY. Oh.

SADIE. Oh dear – here we go…

SADIE *picks up a flyer that's been put through the door.*

ALECKY. Oh – go on.

SADIE. Oh that's bloody… that's Clapton Square who have decided to come and uh have a street party… if we-mm- 'This / is a great chance… This is organised by the community for the community sup*port*ed by Pembury Tenants' and Residents' Association.' You see they should be nothing to do with… Clapton Square. I will see what others // have to say about this.

ALECKY. / Go on, read it out. // Yeah.

Pause.

SADIE (*sotto voce*). Oh God. / (*Beat.*) I do hate all this uh, politics though, sometimes, all the little… it's so annoying isn't it because they have no idea, y'know, they're just not… aware… (*Short pause.*) I might actually just go and see them.

ALECKY. / God – okay.

SADIE. You can't smooth over inequality. You can't say, let's
    meet in-in a street party and talk about the fact that,
    y'know... you're-you're living in quarter-of-a-million-pound
    houses and, uh, y'know, we're struggling to pay our rents.
    It's better for them just to hate the situation and, um, be
    angry about it. I mean maybe one of the most powerful
    things we can do is boycott it, ignore it, actually. Maybe we
    should ignore it. (*Short pause*.) Just completely ignore it and
    set up our own... (*Short pause*.) meeting, another meeting in
    um... (*Short pause*.) I didn't see who put it through actually,
    maybe it was the caretakers who've been leafleting.
    (*Checks*.) Nobody'll go anyway.

SECTION 6 – Tea Party and Stop Criminalising Hackney Youth

26. Radio London

IAN. I said to the BBC TV News that er they should try an' go when we start so they said, 'That's alright, We'll go.'

Phone rings.

Oh this is Anna again, this is from Radio London. Hello?

27. The Whole of the Estate

STEVE. The whole of the estate has been given one of the letters – (*Beat.*) everything it's all done. The whole of this estate, both sides.

28. Muddle

At the tea party on Clarence Road.

SARAH. It's-a – quite a funny atmosphere in here at the moment isn't there?

ALECKY. Yeah, yeah yes it isn't?

SARAH. It could go anyway. No, no they're all cut.

ALECKY. Are they? That one's ever so long.

SARAH. No they're not all cut.

Laughter.

I-I've been in a muddle permanently all week it's just been so nuts. (*Beat.*) I – y'know making really stupid mistakes about everything. Not thinking straight. I'm a real liability.

A bang.

Ooh.

STEVE. There's one.

TONY. There you go.

SARAH. There's the first balloon / burst.

STEVE. / That's one firework.

TONY *giggles*.

29. Worried

IAN. I was gonna say actually I-I-I very silly I'm probably worrying unnecess– I'm worrying y'know we're not gonna get enough local residents coming. Steve Lord told me that they were gonna send round a note round the house-flats 'n' so on. But I'm probably worrying / unnecessarily.

JANE. / Why are you worried about that?

IAN. Well because, y'know, I don't want it to end up with a bunch of onlookers there, actually that'll be exactly the way the riots were actually. / About twenty people actually doing it and everybody else watching but it wi–, y'know, just that we make sure we do get a significant number of local people.

JANE. / Yeah… (*Beat.*) You're not, um, I mean you're not… really worried about this tea party are you?

IAN. I'm just a little bit but I will do I always do worry about things until they're happening 'n' then I'm okay. I'm usually proved wrong as well.

JANE. There'll be Marks and Spencer's cakes, everything'll be fine.

IAN. Yeah.

30. Positive

DOT. As I was sayin' Saturday we're not getting the positive of what's happening on Pembury estate.

IAN. No.

DOT. You're getting all this / media 'n' everyfing –

STEVE. / All – All what ya see is police knocking on the doors, / takin' away the ones who dunnit.

IAN. / Yeah.

DOT. – of all the… all the trouble… y'know we want what's happening positively on the estate not all this…

IAN. No. Hiya Tony.

TONY. Hello there. / You got one a these yeah?

DOT. / I'm on the Residents' Association.

TONY *gives* IAN *a pink and white gingham armband.*

IAN. What's that? Oh, band, oh yes o' course yeah. Um this is Tony / from Clapton Square –

DOT. / Oh, oh hi –

IAN. – Users Group –

DOT. I'm Dot.

TONY. Hi Dot.

DOT. We're on the uh Tenants' / Association of // Pembury –

TONY. / Hi.

IAN. // From Pembury.

TONY. Oh right hi yeah no –

IAN. Yeah yeah so you need to get to know one another.

TONY. Yeah yeah yeah well this… Sarah, my wife runs the uh Clapton Square Users Group.

SARAH (*from afar*). Hi!

DOT. Hi! Go up 'n' introduce myself can I?

SARAH (*in the distance*). Hello.

IAN. Yeah go on. (*Beat*.) That's great.

TONY. Right anyone. Anyone else?

IAN. Um I don't know really.

TONY. I think Sarah needs one.

IAN. I'm-I'm feeling very nervous because, y'know obvious –
the one thing is I-I-I if I was overwhelmed by huge numbers
of local residents I'd be fine, but it's the people who are not
local residents coming, y'know, just because they've heard
about it 'n' they think they're gonna have fun.

31. Young People's Futures

WOMAN IN BARBERS. That will be open today? It's gonna
open today.

COLIN. People worried about the shop, what about young
people's futures? Yeah because the shop will come back but
the-there's more important things than the shop you know?
Th– People's lives. Some kids are gonna get a conviction
that are gonna affect their whole lives, which over moments
of madness. (*Beat*.) You should have went to Tottenham an'
saw Prince Charles was down in Tottenham. And Camilla
was in Tottenham today. They're really working to avoid this
revolution aren't they. They know how serious it is.

32. Interloper

ALAN. Hello there.

IAN. Hi.

ALAN. Hello, how are you?

IAN. Oh hi, how you doing?

ALAN. Nice to see you, how are you?

IAN. Yeah good to see you again, / yeah.

ALAN. / Good. So what's happening?

IAN. There's three lots of BBC here / now… *Newsnight.*

ALAN. / So what's bringing the BBC here today?

IAN. Uh street party. Um… and, uh, but I'm hoping, to be quite frank, that they go away once we start because, we've promised residents that they would not be treated as a spectacle but the idea is to try 'n' talk to one another 'n' if we can start to do that – 'n' in fact I've just introduced, haven't I, someone from the square to somebody from the estate. Two sides of the road 'n' so y'know, people getting to know one another that's what is important.

JANE walks past pushing a trolly with drinks on.

ALAN. Teas and coffees being wheel/ed along?

IAN. / Yeah from Marks and Spencer's now –

ALAN. Is this a tea party?

IAN. Yes it's a tea party but it's coffee as well.

IAN laughs. Beat.

ALAN. It's quite a tricky thing isn't it? Almost being a gatekeeper at this point –

IAN. Yeah.

ALAN. – because you feel a sense of… duty and honour for the community and, the idea of the-the interloper is a complex one isn't it?

IAN. Yeah.

Pause.

ALAN. You're smiling?

IAN. I don't know what you want me to say about that. I mean, who's-who's, I mean, the-I suppose you could turn that question round into – who's who's an outsider? I mean, I – I've lived here all my life, my family have got one hundred and sixty years of tradition living here but I also think it's really important to-to welcome people. I was civic mayor, uh, three years ago and, uh, wearing the chain and going around, and sometimes you-people used to say to me: you

don't sound like somebody from Hackney, be-be-that's
because, when I was brought up, my mum and dad wanted
me to speak proper. But the important thing is that there are
lots of people who do speak in different ways, they speak
posh, they speak because they're-in a-in a Vietnamese way,
they speak in an Afro-Caribbean way, however-however they
speak it's all just about recognising that we're all people and
neighbours here together, that we all belong here as far as
I'm concerned. If you're living here, for a few days, and you
belong with us 'n' it's part of our community 'n' we will
fight for you if we have to 'n' we'll defend you if we have to.

33. Not Their Story

On the estate away from the party.

KATE. *I* don't think Clapton Square have *any* i*dea* what life is
like, or has been like, for these young people on that estate at
all. And-and it's like apartheid. (*Beat*.) It's completely like
apartheid. And it is almost like, y'know, uuum, from-from
the days of the Vic*tori*an sort of 'well we're step over into
the sort of y'know 'n' be seen to be doing a little bit of
good'. Well it's not-it's not good enough. To throw a tea
party on Clarence Road, how many young people want to go
to that? What pisses me off more than *any*thing else is when
they start quoting 'oh it's so dangerous, to ho we can't…'
you know, and I had such a go at this woman, who was so
posh you wouldn't believe, she was saying 'oh but you know
I must warn Jamie's girlfriend about this' and I went mad. I
said 'd'you think she's' – (*Beat*.) about being shot, because
somebody's been – a young person had been shot, and she's
'oh my God that's terrible I must warn blah blah blah.' I said
do you think she, is under any threat of being shot or
stabbed? (*Beat*.) How many young, white, middle-class
people get shot or stabbed round here? None. Do you know
what I mean? And how people want to get on that
bandwagon and turn it in to their own fucking project.
*Abs*olutely drives me nuts, y'know, cos it's *not*, it's not their
story. It is not. Their. Story. It's all in the abstract for them
isn't it? Because it happens around them, not to them.

34. Solidarity

SADIE. We got some money from Hackney Trades Council, got two hundred quid from them 'n' / they've backed it.

KATE. / Oh that's good. And what about the cards and y'know the information re: y'know, young people's thoughts 'n' and –

SADIE. Oh we-we've got / a leaflet –

KATE. / Have you got-got any?

SADIE. – 'n' po– can you put a po/ster up?

KATE. We can you put one up. Yeah definitely.

SADIE. Yeah. (*Pause*.) You know what I really want I want people to come Sunday, and I've got tickets an' hardly anybody has, committed to coming on that / coach.

KATE. / I can't – I'm going away, yeah um –

SADIE. But, last week's meeting was quite small / but, um, you know –

KATE. / Okay.

SADIE. – I think it was a shame because we had something to tell them we had the, posters and we had the leaflets and we had, er, the money from the Trades Council.

KATE. Right.

SADIE. Um, and there's still loads of things to do I mean. Um – (*Exhales*.) but the-the thing is now is con– getting those families to contact us and start building a support network –

KATE. Hm.

SADIE. – and start, / y'know, making people aware that these things have happened –

KATE. / Hm.

SADIE. – y'know –

KATE. Hm.

SADIE. – that these kids have been arrested, what an injustice –

KATE. I kno-know, I know it's so true –

SADIE. – y'know, y'know –

KATE. – it's absolutely true.

SADIE. – um but no we can't do anything unless we –

KATE. No I know well –

SADIE. – get the stories. It's just about getting people together isn't it and going right ya know –

KATE. It's about solidarity isn't it Sadie.

SADIE. – We're all in this together. We're not we just need all these mums / involved.

KATE. / I know it's *so* difficult getting them to sort of, y'know, / some of them just like are not, I mean they're not like me // y'know –

SADIE. / Yeah. // No.

KATE. 'N' I don't say that in a good or a bad way but just that they-they don't have any sort of interest. All they want is, I guess, y'know they don't want the aggravation, they don't want their sons to be locked up 'n' when it's over it's just like… y'know, some of them don't even go to court to be honest it is just…

ALECKY. Really?

KATE. Yeah. There's a boy who's now still in prison, through four court appearances not one mem– family member turned up. It's heartbreaking. / Maybe that's the way he wants it. // I don't know.

SADIE. / Yeah but… // But we would've turned up. (*Pause.*) What we need to do now, it goes back to the issues that caused it in the first place.

KATE. Yeah.

SADIE. It goes back to / all the stuff about stop and search and dispersals and that's what the campaign i-i- you know.

KATE. / Yes. Yes it does, it does. It does, it completely does.

SADIE. Yeah we need to tr– you know, tr– I know it's really hard to get young people involved but, it's like well –

KATE. It would, y'know...

SADIE. – it to break it, y'know?

KATE. I know, no I know, I know. Um... I mean y'know I just wish my son would because he's –

SADIE. – He could be-he could be leading this campaign –

KATE. He could, he absolutely could.

SADIE. – And I'd rather he did.

Laughter.

KATE. He abso– No, honestly Sadie, he absolutely could.

Pause.

SADIE. But yeah come along to the meeting tonight.

KATE. Yeah.

SADIE. Yeah. Coz like ye-yeah, I get a bit kind of like, if not many people are coming I get kind of like 'there's no point' / and um –

KATE. / No you have to be I'll have a check to see if I can conjure up some more interest. I'll have another go at Raph, I'll have another go at Raph. Lovely to see you.

ALECKY. Thanks Kate, okay bye.

KATE *leaves.*

Pause.

SADIE. But it's good you know, at least she understands that she needs to actually come to meetings.

ALECKY. Yep. Yep.

SADIE. Because there's no point having all this passion an' anger if you can't channel it into something. You know, that's the whole point isn't it.

ALECKY. Exactly.

SADIE. You-you-you're completely, you know, united you stand divided you fall.

ALECKY. Exactly.

Pause.

SADIE. I've got a questionnaire to design. (*Beat.*) To be honest I've got better things to do, I shouldn't say that because I haven't got better things to do but I'm, I really am a bit worried about work. Maybe I just need to get myself a bit more organised really.

ALECKY. Yeah.

SADIE. Eighty people put their names down to be active campaigners, / but it's actually when it comes to doing something // so it's like, 'Right now I'll go and hand out these leaflets', and we haven't even got any posters up.

ALECKY. / Yes. // Yes.

SADIE. But I think that everybody likes to have a leader, don't they. And they think that you're going to do everything.

ALECKY. Yes.

SADIE. Ya know. They don't realise how much time it takes.

ALECKY. No I know, yeah.

SADIE. And of cour– it's about, if nobody's interested then I'm not interested either because there's no point.

ALECKY. No, exactly.

35. Hello Priest

Back at the party the street is now full of people. Techno music plays. Children draw on the pavements in colourful chalk and HULA-HOOP GIRLS *and locals dance to the music.*

HULA-HOOP GIRL. Hello darling how are you? / Hi. Hello priest.

FATHER ROB. / Very good.

MAN WITH CAKE. They're trying to get the community back together again.

36. Pasties

DEANNE *stands just outside* COLIN*'s barber's.*

Music and laughter.

DEANNE. How you doing? (*Beat.*) Come and have a drink. Ha ha ha ha. (*Beat.*) I just congratulated Marks and Spencer's. (*Laughter.*) I asked dem if they brought that special cake that I like with the cream in it y'know the ones we can use for birthdays 'n' he said no but every other cake is there. (*Laughter.*) I said will you have any pasties out there he said, 'You don't want much!' I said, 'No I don't want much.' (*Laughter through nose.*) It's well done, it's good it's good. Some people are suspicious, mind you. I've heard de rumours going on dat uh – (*Sigh.*) they want to get faces from people on the community, the young people for somebody to have it lined up 'n' say 'oh um… *dat* one was dere and *dis* one was dere'. But they said the youth are more smarter than that.

37. Celebrity

LUKE'S MUM. Celebrity!

LUKE. Yeah.

LUKE'S MUM. Cos you know you can nominate someone to carry the Olympic flag – er the Olympic torch. Well we're gonna nominate him!

38. Feeling Good

SIVA. We're feeling good. Opening today that's all we waited for. Hello Jane how are you?

JANE. Look at you, how are you?

SIVA. Not bad darling.

JANE. Bigger smile than ever.

SIVA. Of *course* / this is all you waited for.

JANE. / How-d… How'd you feel?

SIVA. Ah I feel *very* good / y'know, ve– I can't express myself y'know. That day I was cried.

JANE. / Oh!

Laughter.

SIVA. Today I'm laughing.

JANE (*laughter*). Yeah.

SIVA. Oh. Very happy than have anything else.

39. Don't Be Such a Creep!

SARAH. Can I just say you're missing some quality chat over here.

ALECKY. Oh dooooh– Really. Really? / – okay good well done. Thank you. Can I drop in on the conversation – were you // sharing your thoughts on Hackney?

SARAH. / Yeah. Yeah.

MC POWER. // Okay. I was MC Power
An' I was givin' – showin' this flower
That I do this every hour,
I can do thi' in my sleep
I can do it when I'm weak.

TONY. Hmm.

ALECKY giggles. MC POWER laughs.

MC POWER. You need to change / that laugh.

TONY. / That is fantastic.

ALECKY. Ha ha. That's brilliant.

MC POWER. Yeah. It's all good.

ALECKY. That's brilliant. Can you do one about the riots?

SARAH laughs. ALECKY cackles.

ALECKY. Please. Especially Siva's shop. Can you jus' do something about that?

MC POWER. I… feel it for the guy wid da shop
He got his shop looted 'n' they took a lot
They took all his wines 'n' they took all his spirit
But I'm the guy that, like the Holy Spirit
I'm come to h-help out
I have to scream, I have to shout
What was all that really about?

Beat.

I'm Mr MC Power
And I'm still come at this hour
And the lady I'm looking at she's like a flower
So I can't look into her eye too deep
Because it makes me wanna go home 'n' sleep.

Laughter.

SARAH. No man surely I make / you wanna weep!

TONY. / Weep.

ALECKY. Weep! Weep! / Weep, not sleep!

MC POWER. / Yeah.

SARAH. It's all going wrong if I'm making you wanna sleep man.

Laughter.

MC POWER. Pleeeeaze! Okay.

Beat.

TONY. You can't say that she's cheap.

Laughter.

SARAH. Little / Bo-Peeps.

ALECKY. / Don't be such a creep.

TONY. / Not. Not sleek.

Yeah.

MC POWER. Don't be such a creep!
But I'm not here to / defeat.

JANE. / I've got some news to tell you, sorry, guess what it's got up to now as of an hour ago, twenty th– sorry I've lost it – (*Looking on her iPhone*.) twenty-five thousand three hundred and thirty-three pounds and fifty-four pence.

Cheers.

40. Middle Class

ALECKY. It's good – / go–...

SARAH. / I-I I'm really slightly concerned that we / might –

ALECKY. / What?

SARAH. – That we might be the worst possible / sounding middle class.

TONY. / Hmmm. Hmmm.

ALECKY. No no no no. / No. I mean I'm sort of interested at looking at that that tension but I'm really not tryin' to ss–

TONY. / No cos I think it's what what we were jus' saying there... I think we're also genuinely going into the community and that is sort of, ya know-I think that's – doesn't matter what class you are. / I'm proud to be middle class. I'm white and middle class – that's what I am. Ya know so d– I have no concerns about being seen as that. But ya know it's what we do that matters.

ALECKY. / Yeah you're.

Exactly, don't worry, I'm not going to stitch you up. /

SARAH *laughs nervously.*

Okay? Okay? Okay? I mean she will obviously have to have flowers in her hair and plaits. // But ha ha ha.

TONY. / Yeah, no we know – actually ya know I-I-I –

SARAH. // Yeah. Yeah, yeah, yeah.

TONY. But I – cos ya know, I jus sort of always been ya know proud to be middle class. (*Beat*.) Food's much better!

ALECKY *and* SARAH *laugh raucously.* TONY *chuckles*.

ALECKY. That's going in. (*Referring to her Dicataphone*.)

More laughter.

SARAH. I can't help being middle class. / That – ya know that that's who who – that's I am.

ALECKY. / No not – me too. Exactly we cannot help our our / being –

TONY. / That's who I am. Yeah that's who I am.

ALECKY. I'm the same.

SARAH. What I'm interested in is the – the spaces between people who've come from very different backgrounds and how do you bridge those gaps, how do you knit a community together? How do you face-to-face meet – someone else, how do you – how do you understand someone who's different to you – how do you connect with that person?

41. Cupcakes and Pick Them Out

COLIN. S'alright, this is all lots of strangers, this not local people. (*Pause*.) I can't even… oh one. Two. Three. Four. (*Pause*.) Four local people I've seen. (*Chuckle*.) That I've known he he – no – five, lemme see. From here I can only see about five local people. (*Pause*.) Something wrong here. Isn't it? (*Pause*.) They probably want more than just tea and cakes innit? They want solutions ha ha ha. Huh? They need more, they need a youth centre, or they need something else but they don't need a tea party. Eh? (*Chuckle*.) From Marks and Spencer's. He's a Marks and Spencer's employee. (*Giggles*.) Did you know Marks and Spencer's were providing all this?

M & S EMPLOYEE. Oh – no I-I recognise some of the cupcakes. / With the icing on the top. Quite nice. I think it's good yeah, yeah, there's quite a lot of stuff out on the spread today. Yeah just to, just to give back I guess, just to settle stuff.

COLIN. / Ha.

Or is it to attract, or is it to attract the looters? They like free fings.

Laughter.

It's could be a big steal isn't it?

Laughter.

They been picking them out one by one, with no bail. (*Pause*.) They may be someone's child that you know. (*Chuckle*.) You can't do that.

42. Rubbish

LUKE'S MUM. In one way I'm glad it happened because it's woken everybody up.

LUKE. 'N' it's got rid a the rubbish.

LUKE'S MUM. Yeah it has got rid of all the shit round here now.

LUKE. No because they know now if they start, they will evict 'em. Cos they dunnit, they came on to 'n' start 'n' started evicting people for it.

LUKE'S MUM. They got all their pictures up, everyone's that was involved they've arrested 'n' evicted their parents. Yeah. It's in the tenancy agreement, if you cause anyfing like that you're out yeah so they'd all be gone. Yerr. We got a mobile police station at the bottom of the Hindrey Road 'n' all the ones that the – wiv the cameras they got pictures of *all* of 'em 'n' they go through all the pictures, everyone they find they're evicting their parents. All the pictures are there 'n' everyfing they're gettin 'em all out. (*Beat*.) Good. That's what we like. A bitta peace and quiet round here.

43. Pentonville

DEANNE. I wanted – I was looking for Desiree because her so[n]-her-her, um, nephew got arrested on in the riots? Y'know he's in Pentonville? Imagine? (*Kisses teeth.*) Yeah. Because I went to find out what the hell was going on, plus that night he had his head bust as well 'n' I wondered if the police was looking about him. Dey won't even tell us what 'n' what for. He's on remand they haven't even got to him yet. They haven't even – they HAVEN'T even got to him yet. They DON'T KNOW nothing… it's not fair. Society is not fair, the government is not fair. They're just holding him so you make sure you write that down. They're just holding him.

44. Income Creation Scheme

TONY. Guy who, um, hangs around sort of down, on the Narrow Way and y'know, he's, he always se– asks me for money and y'know, every so often I'll give him fifty pee or a quid – he ran up to me and sort of y'know put a coupla quid in my hand and said that's for the fund and I just sort of thought, oh ya know I just sort of I said sort of – (*Laughter.*) I started to cry… sort of like I just thought what an amazing thing to do ya know I-I-I just thought God that's a really incredibly sort of strong sort of y'know, um, sort of thing of the community we live in. Course it's also y'know brilliant income-creation scheme now because every time I see him y'know I reach into my pockets cos sort of like just think oh what an amazing gesture, what a great guy, y'know.

45. Guesstimate, Street Art, Reclaiming the Streets

FATHER ROB. I think it's been an extraordinary success today. We think there's been somewhere between um three and four hundred, if not more here er-today. That's a-that's a the kinda guesstimate figures which Marks and Spencer's have been pulling together. Erm 'n' so that's, y'know really pleased to

see that uh, that taking place. Yeah I'm pleased. I just
thought I love the-the-the things that are on the-on the
pavements as well, the street art 'n' stuff. Of course it's
gonna rain which means it'll all wash away. I was-I was I
was praying big time for rain last Monday night that's what I
was doing. Because actually if we had-ha– a kind of massive
outburst the whole thing would've dissipated 'n' people
woulda gone home. But there we go.

JANE. But you know it is jus-just that thing, reclaiming the
streets isn't it? Last time there was a gathering of people it
was a really nasty gathering of people wasn't it?

46. We Did It, We Did, We Did It!

R & B music plays.

IAN. It's absolutely brilliant but I-uh with these things I'm
always kinda like reasonably passive and I sit down at home
and I suddenly it's: yeah! Did it, did it, did it, did it yeah!

*Teasing a child who is drawing on the pavement in coloured
chalks.*

Did you write here? You know it's against the law to write
on the pavement?

IAN *dances to the beats.*

47. Muffins

CHRISTOPH. Well that was impressive but I don't think they
did it just for uh for uh for the community, they did it for uh
for PR reasons, that's what I think. (*Beat.*) Um my name is
Christoph, I'm a reporter for uh *Der Spiegel* magazine. It's
still great, it's still uh lovely that everybody came together
on the street but uh the people I talked to, uhm from-from
Pembury, they were very suspicious. Uh and either they
carried away muffins to their homes so they wouldn't stay

here and didn't dr– um drink tea with – with the other
people, or um they would just say it-it's ridiculous, we-we
don't need this, we don't need-we don't need muffins to be
given to, we're not-we're not uh… *star*ving here. Um, you
see a lot of… um… issues uh… on this street… um…
uhm… where I-where I think you can tell, uh, a lot of things
about British society – because um there are a lot of hip and
young people, that's uh urban London, wearing, um, very
short jeans er with bare ankles, no socks, um uh and-uh, um
have really poor people on the other side of the street.

48. Front Cover

TONY. Have you seen that? I-I wondered if that's ever
happened before? Opening your newspaper shop when
you're on the front cover of the newspaper. That's uh, really
poignant isn't it? Ha ha ha. (*Beat. To* CHRISTOPH.) I'm
Tony, hi. Nice to meet you.

SARAH. We've had a lot of German uh… / journalists.

TONY. / Yeah a lot / of German interest.

CHRISTOPH. / I know I know I bumped into-into them,
every… fff / thirty minutes.

SARAH. / Why, why, cos we've had the odd one from
elsewhere in Europe, why so many Germans, why is it such
a big story there?

CHRISTOPH. Flights are cheap?

Beat. Laughter.

SARAH. Okay yeah. / Okay.

COMMUNITY CHORUS. / Good answer.

TONY. Ha ha. Yeah.

CHRISTOPH. Um…

TONY. And the euro's strong, yeah. Let's face it.

CHRISTOPH. An' the euro's very strong / yeah.

TONY. / Yeah.

SARAH. Yeah.

CHRISTOPH. Yeah.

TONY. / That'll be…

CHRISTOPH. / No to be honest, to be honest the weather is really bad in Germany right now.

   SARAH *laughs*.

TONY. Really?

49. Naff

SADIE. Helloo.

ALECKY. Hello!

SADIE. Alright.

   Pause.

ALECKY. Ian, this is Sadie. Sadie this is…

SADIE. Hello Ian. / Nice to meet you.

IAN. / Hiya.

ALECKY. This is Ian Rathbone.

SADIE. Hello.

IAN. Hello.

ALECKY. This is Steve.

IAN. Steve.

SADIE. I know Steve / oh I do-I do know…

ALECKY. / Oh you know Steve… you know yeah, I guess you know the…

SADIE. From quite a long long time ago.

ALECKY *laughs awkwardly.*

Yeah I want to um, share with you information about a,
another campaign that's started, just started so we've just had
our very first meeting. I mean I-I-I'm I have to say one of the
– ya know – just to get it out there / – is y'know possibly lots
of – lots of people loved the street party, but there were like
other voices as well that um… thought it, y'know, was a bit…

IAN. / Mmm. (*Pause.*) Naff?

Pause.

SADIE. Yeah. 'N' I'm just being really honest –

IAN. No. That's valid.

SADIE. I would have thought it would have been, led and
organised by the Tenants' Association.

IAN. A lot of people said they liked the street party 'n' they
wanted to do it again, I said over my dead body ya know –
(*Laughter.*) because the organisation of it was incredible. But
I think it's really important that the street's people, to put it
very crudely, and the estate people should see themselves as
part of the same area, y'know, it's Clarence Road has got
two sides to it –

SADIE. It has.

IAN. – and I mean the Clapton Square Users Group, uh, who,
um, who are fairly well-off, middle-class professional people
have realised that they might need to do something more 'n'
they're gonna meet with Steve, I-I don't think they've sorted
anything out yet?

STEVE. No.

IAN. But they're gonna meet with them to discuss issues.

SADIE. There's lots of issues.

STEVE. Th– / This stop-and-search thing, right, I I-my p-
personal opinion I think it's a good idea. I know, I know for
a fact what was, what had been found / on this estate, right –
machetes, knives you know, things like this, er, // bayonets,
er, spears, /// guns in them bushes, //// er, bullets hidden
behind, ///// er, posted tissue.

SADIE. / Okay. // Yeah. /// Yeah. //// Mmmm. ///// Yeah.

You know I'm not saying nobody's saying those things don't happen. But we're, you know, you've even / just –

STEVE. / I see – I see the children on here and there's mothers over there that swear blind, they're so religious their child don't do nothing. They wanna see what their child does in Clarence Road. If I got one on the side I'd give them such a good hiding round the corner he'd wonder what day of the week it was.

IAN. But you can't do that Steve.

STEVE. But you can. The police can do it as well, when they're not, er, watched. (*Beat.*) We've got to go back to the old policing days, you...

SADIE. / But you're way out of touch, this is the problem –

IAN. / But you can't go... Hold on hold, hold on –

STEVE. – We coming out-we coming out of it but we, eventually we'll end up having to be –

SADIE. / I'm gonna go.

IAN. / Okay well um...

STEVE. – like America and our police will have to carry guns because now, we have got the criminals of the world coming to this country. (*Beat.*) Everything you try to do on this estate. / People just – it's just a waste of time people don't wanna know.

DOT. / Waste of time. If it isn't right in their face, they don't wanna know.

STEVE. They just don't wanna know. / (*Beat.*) And then when you get an issue // about the youth – this what gets me, /// right – *every*body wants to jump up 'n' say 'oh them poor little boys how they're treated, mistreated' –

IAN. / Yeah. // Yeah. /// Yeah.

SADIE. Because they care about –

STEVE. Don't get me wrong –

SADIE. Because they care about young people, their families.

STEVE. It don't matter, I, my kids were born on this estate –

DOT. So was mine.

STEVE. Forty years I've been on this estate / right? –

SADIE. / Yeah.

STEVE. – Forty years 'n' there was never ever any problems like there is now on this estate. 'N' you can't tell me it's down to not having jobs, this, that 'n' the other, there's plenty of opportunities for people to do stuff on this estate 'n', y'know –

SADIE. What's it down to then, whadda you think?

STEVE. I-i-it's down the way they're brought up. The parents – / I blame the parents, I blame the parents I really blame the parents, because they don't care what their children do. Right? 'N' as, as far as the-the ASBOs were concerned or whatever they are, the uh –

DOT. / The family life. The parents!

IAN. Dispersal zone?

STEVE. Dispersal zone, / I think it was a great idea, I really do, I really believe that because these elderly people down here, not one of them will now come out after five o'clock in the evening. They're too scared. They're too scared. This man here had a man put away for threatening to shoot him. // Right and what did he do? Kill-kill four people in Amhurst Road in shops round there.

IAN. / Yeah.

SADIE. // I know you've had particular issues.

Anyway I'm not here uhm to criticise you, but you know you have said some quite extreme things, I think.

STEVE. But that is, that is my opinion. (*Chuckles*.)

SADIE. I'm gonna go. Yeah.

IAN. Still leafleting. Anyway, look listen listen. / It's been interesting.

STEVE. / I've done my leafleting.

ALECKY. Mmm.

SADIE. This'll be my daughter coz she hasn't got a key. Sorry.

IAN. Yeah. Okay. Yep. / Well that's…

SADIE. / I'm gonna go. Thank you so much for your time.

STEVE. That's alright. Okay.

SADIE. Thank you.

SECTION 7 – Shop Opens

50. Open

STEVE. You alright? / Ooh, it's come undone.

SIVA. / Yes, very good.

JANE. Whoops the ribbon's come undone.

IAN. Okay. I think probably people are gonna have to stand
back a bit to allow the photographers to take their pictures.

OFFICIAL PHOTOGRAPHER. Right, guys…

IAN. Erm Siv! Right you say your bit, then I'll say my bit and
that'll be it yeah?

IAN *addresses the crowd assembled outside the shop.*

As the-as the chair of the Friends of Siva erm campaign I just
wanted to say something uh, sort of on a human level because
this – this is about human beings responding to other human
beings in need of love and care 'n' I really take my hat off to
the Friends of Siva who are here today 'n' all the community
in this area who have given so much and continue to be so
kind. This is more than a shop it's a bridge –

A local puts some money into a collection bucket.

– between, there we are –

JANE. More money, / money coming in.

IAN. / More money, there you are.

Laughter.

I'll look after it for him. It's just clear this is more than a
shop, as shops so often are, it's a bridge between
communities here. It's a place where you can meet others
you may not usually meet / – and it's a place where there is
friendliness and kindliness – you know that cos you're a
customer aren't you. //

GUEST SHOPKEEPER. / Mmmm… // It's true.

LOCAL. Yeah.

GUEST SHOPKEEPER. No I'm a shopkeeper.

Laughter.

IAN. Okay so you would say that wouldn't you? So it's a sharing together isn't it? / And so to say thank you to the local community for all that they've done here and this is just the start.

SIVA. / Yes of course.

Applause.

Somebody, she, old lady, she gave me this card with the pension, and her money £150.

SARAH. Wow.

SIVA. Serious, I'm not lying. Just it-it just, y'know you don't see how much people are l–, y'know they love me. / Probably, y'know, a few people, they hate –

Laughter from the crowd.

– me but hundreds of – hundreds and thousands of people love me all over the place.

SARAH. / Yeah.

IAN. Okay so I declare the shop, open.

Cheers. Clapping.

SIVA. Aw, thank you.

GUEST SHOPKEEPER. So pleased for you.

SARAH. Lead the way.

OFFICIAL PHOTOGRAPHER. Siva? Just before you go, can we have a picture of your family –

SIVA. Yeah.

OFFICIAL PHOTOGRAPHER. – and the local people –

SIVA. Yeah.

OFFICIAL PHOTOGRAPHER. – outside your shop.

SIVA. Yeah no problem…

EPILOGUE

51. Do You Remember Me?

ALECKY (*bursting in loudly, out of breath*). Hello? / It's Colin isn't it?

COLIN. / Hello.

Yes it is.

ALECKY. Do you remember me from like making my play about the riots?

COLIN. Oh yeah.

ALECKY. Huh. (*Getting her breath back.*) *Hi.*

COLIN. You sort of disappeared. I never saw you again.

ALECKY. I know I did disappear for a bit. Can I talk to you a bit more?

COLIN. About what?!

ALECKY. Well I'll tell you why –

COLIN. What d'you want? Skin or just a number one?

SKIN CLIENT. That's fine just skin.

Sound of the clippers.

COLIN. Skin?

SKIN CLIENT. Yeah.

COLIN. Okay.

ALECKY. – Uhm because they're about to say on the news whether, I thought it was quite a pertinent time to come back because I think at about half past three the jury's gonna conclude on whether the police uhm were guilty of like killing Mark Duggan.

Beat.

COLIN. Okay.

ALECKY. Erm. So I sort of wondered whether – I didn't know whether you'd be listening to it on the radio ya see that's all.

COLIN. No. I didn't realise it was – I didn't realise it was gonna be there.

ALECKY. Yeah, just basically I heard it on the radio in my studio and I-they said they're gonna do it in half an hour and I was like 'Oh!' I wanted to come and chat to you again anyway because you were a really good – voice in it. You're kind of like the voice of like lot of people who come in here I sort of felt.

COLIN. Okay.

ALECKY. So erm, yeah. / Can we. Do you get? –

COLIN. / What er?

ALECKY. Wher– Cos they might announce it like – do you see what I mean? Like on BBC News or whatever.

COLIN. On BBC News?

ALECKY. Yeah.

COLIN. Eh, I'll see.

He goes over to his radio. The CUSTOMER *looks unimpressed by this intrusion.*

ALECKY. Oh brilliant. (*Beat.*) I'm sorry to kind of invade in all of a fluster but I was like 'Oh!'

Music plays as COLIN *fiddles with the dial.*

It'll probably be on Beeb – on the radio.

Voice of a radio presenter as COLIN *continues to scan.*

COLIN. Oh… right.

Jingle plays, 'BBC Radio / 2.'

ALECKY. / That's twooo.

COLIN. Yer-errr.

Music blares.

ALECKY (*becoming impatient*). What do you normally listen to radio-wise?

COLIN. I wonder whether / this is –

ALECKY. / If not have you got BBC or Sky News.

COLIN. Errrr. (*Goes to his TV.*) I wonder if it's on there.

ALECKY. Huh… Oh… No… No… No. (*Long pause as he flicks through the channels.*) Ah – yes yes!! The one before.

COLIN. Alright.

ALECKY. Yes! (*Beat.*) Okay.

BEN GAGIN (*on TV*). And a majority say lawful killing with two of the jurers saying there is an open conclusion and there are cries of 'No!' from the Duggan family / in here this afternoon and the jury –

COLIN. / Ya see 'lawful killing' it was always going to be that decision anyway.

On the TV scenes of family members and supporters outside court shouting down the police spokesman reading out the press statement.

ALECKY. Yeah. Oh dear, it's the police now.

COLIN. Yes.

More shouting.

He best give up innit.

SKIN CLIENT. The people are not happy. How can they reach that verdict?

More shouting of 'Murderer, murderer, murderer!'

ALECKY. Oh my word.

COLIN *gets back to work. The sound of his clippers and the yelling TV makes it difficult to hear his speech.*

COLIN. They're not, they're not, they're not letting him.
There's got to be a better, a better, a better way instead of
rioting y'know to handle them like that innit? Ha ha. He
cannot be heard. / He cannot defend it. He has to go on a
programme where there's no interruption isn't it. No one's
hearing what he's saying. But they didn't hear the people's
voice in the first place so why should they hear his voice.
(*Beat.*) Poor man has to go home to his wife after all of that.
Ha ha ha ha he he.

SKIN CLIENT. / Can't get his words out.

*The yelling on the TV and sound of the clippers build into a
crescendo.*

End.

www.nickhernbooks.co.uk

facebook.com/nickhernbooks

twitter.com/nickhernbooks